Christos Yannaras

Christos Yannaras
The Apophatic Horizon of Ontology

Basilio Petrà

Translated by
Norman Russell

James Clarke & Co

James Clarke & Co
P.O. Box 60
Cambridge
CB1 2NT
United Kingdom

www.jamesclarke.co
publishing@jamesclarke.co

Hardback ISBN: 978 0 227 17704 4
Paperback ISBN: 978 0 227 17703 7
PDF ISBN: 978 0 227 90703 0
ePub ISBN: 978 0 227 90704 7
Kindle ISBN: 978 0 227 90705 4

British Library Cataloguing in Publication Data
A record is available from the British Library

First published by James Clarke & Co, 2019

Copyright © Editrice Morcelliana, 2015
English translation © Basilio Petrà, 2019

Original work: Basilio Petrà, *Christos Yannaras*
(Brescia: Editrice Morcelliana, 2015)

All rights reserved. No part of this edition may be reproduced, stored electronically or in any retrieval system, or transmitted in any form or by any means, electronic, mechanical, photocopying, recording, or otherwise, without prior written permission from the Publisher (permissions@jamesclarke.co).

Contents

Introduction   vii

Chapter I   1
The Discovery of Russian Orthodoxy: the West as a Problem

    1. From Orthodox Pietism to the Discovery of Personalism and Russian Orthodoxy

    2. Dostoevsky's Criticism of the West and the Mission of Orthodoxy

Chapter II   15
The Encounter with Heidegger and the Ontological Hermeneutic of the West: the Way of Apophaticism

    1. Heidegger and the Nihilistic Outcome of Western Metaphysics: the Way beyond Nihilism; Eastern Apophaticism

    2. Yannaras' 'Conversion to Ontology' and the Discovery of the Ontological Difference with the West: the Rediscovery of 'Greek Metaphysics' and Its Connection with Apophaticism

    3. Eastern Apophaticism and Orthodox Apologetics: the Gnoseological Topicality of Apophaticism and Its Iconological Character

Chapter III   34
From the Personalist Ontology of the Fathers to a Critical Ontology: between Theology and Philosophy

    1. *Person and Eros*: a Theological Essay in Post-Heideggarian Ontology

    2. A Hermeneutic Interval

3. The Philosophical Elaboration of a 'Critical Ontology': the Possibility of an 'Apophatic Rationalism': the Social Fruitfulness of Apophaticism

  4. *Propositions of a Critical Ontology*: a 'Revisionist Empiricism'

CHAPTER IV   71
The Development of Reflection on Critical Ontology

  1. From *Person and Eros* to *What Can Be Said and What Cannot Be Said*: the Second 'Fundamental Stage' in Yannaras' thought

  2. Relational Ontology

CHAPTER V   81
Ontology and Salvation

  1. Introductory Considerations

  2. *Thrēskeiopoiēsē*: Religion and the Ontological Distortion of Christianity

  3. *Against Religion*: Natural Religion, the Religious Transformation of Christianity and the Reshaping of the Church.

Epilogue   92

Christos Yannaras: The Communal Verification of Knowledge   93

  1. The Genesis of Critical Thought

  2. Truth as *Mode*

  3. Correct Thinking (*Orthōs Dianoeisthai*) through Correctly Sharing in Common (*Orthōs Koinōnein*)

  4. A Shared Empiricism

  5. Symbol

  6. Apophaticism

  7. The Historical Eclipse of Apophaticism

  8. The Embodiment of Apophaticism in a Culture

  9. The Counterfeiting of the Ancient Greek Enterprise

  10. Gnoseology Differentiates Cultures

Bibliography   113

Index   127

Introduction

The aim of this book is to serve as an introduction to the thought of Christos Yannaras,[1] one of the most important Orthodox thinkers of the second half of the twentieth century and the beginning of the present millennium.

His role has been – and still is – extraordinarily significant in Greece, where he has radically renewed the cultural perception of religious discourse by the force and novelty of his thinking and by the style of his linguistic expression.[2] He has an imposing presence on the Greek cultural scene. It is no exaggeration to say that one can easily distinguish between pre-Yannaras and post-Yannaras theology in Greece, between theology as an academic discipline and theology as a passion for the fullness of life, for victory over death.

Briefly, his work has had vast repercussions in Orthodoxy as a whole, in the various Orthodox national churches. His works have been translated into Russian, Romanian, Serbian, Bulgarian, Ukrainian and Finnish; and a great number of them also into English, Italian, French and German.

---

1. The author's name and surname (in transliteration *Chrēstos Giannaras*) are given here in the form by which they are known internationally. The same principle is adopted with regard to all the names of Greek authors. In every other case, however, I transcribe the Greek text in Latin characters. With regard to pronunciation, the accentuation is thus: Chrístos Yannarás.
2. Yannaras was the first Greek theologian to use *dimotiki* or popular Greek as his normal language, abandoning the *katharevousa* or 'purified' Greek that was the official language of academic theology, of the Church and of the state.

On the international and ecumenical levels Yannaras is considered to be among the most eminent representatives of Orthodox thought, sometimes the subject of controversy and debate, but, nonetheless, always listened to with attention, respect and gratitude. For about ten years he was a member of the editorial board of the well-known international theological journal, *Concilium*.

As a result, one might think that the value and importance of Yannaras' work is more theological and ecclesial than philosophical. In fact, that is not the case. Indeed, in Yannaras, as to a very large extent in the rest of Orthodox thinking in the twentieth century, it is not easy to distinguish between theological and philosophical thought. From the beginning of his reflection the ontological question has been fundamental, that is to say, what has been most important has been an essentially philosophical problem,[3] a problem that nevertheless for Yannaras not only does not separate philosophy from theological thought but constitutes a point of contact between the two fields of knowledge, especially in the case of Christian theological thought because in its Christian form salvation has an ontological content and structure.[4]

As a theologian and also a philosopher Yannaras therefore constitutes a special way of entering into Greek Orthodox self-consciousness and its specific capacity for responding to the challenges of modernity and post-modernity. The Greek character of this self-consciousness should be emphasised because the whole of Yannaras' thought constitutes a powerful intellectual force for maintaining the idea of Hellenism's role in Christianity and of Hellenism itself as an adequate cultural container because through it Christianity has the possibility of expressing the truth of God and of Man in Christ in a fitting manner.

---

3. The accusation that Yannaras is a theologian and not a philosopher was at the centre of the controversy that arose from his success in the competition for the chair in philosophy at the Panteion University of Athens. He has responded to this accusation on various occasions, noting that 'the *ontological* content of a concept (from whatever cognitive object such a concept derives) is a philosophical problem, because ontology constitutes a heading or a branch of systematic philosophy which is not to be identified with any heading or branch even of systematic theology' (Christos Yannaras, *Kritikes Parembaseis* [Critical Interventions] [Athens: Domos, 1983], p. 96).
4. It is not by chance that the international congress on Christos Yannaras, organised by ORTF (Orthodox Theological Research Forum) at St Edmund's Hall, Oxford, England (2-5 September 2013), bore the title, *Christos Yannaras: Philosophy, Theology, Culture*.

CHAPTER I

The Discovery of Russian Orthodoxy: the West as a Problem

1. From Orthodox Pietism to the Discovery of Personalism and of Russian Orthodoxy

Christos Yannaras was born in Athens in 1935. At the age of eighteen, on completing his secondary education, he entered the Orthodox theological brotherhood *Zōē* (Life) which at that time was extremely influential in Greek society and numbered among its most prestigious members Panayiotis Trembelas, a prolific professor of Orthodox dogmatics in the Faculty of Theology of the University of Athens.

Yannaras remained a member of this brotherhood for almost ten years, becoming one of its most dynamic younger members.[1] He left it only after a long inner struggle, in 1964, and dedicated himself for some years to philosophical and theological studies in his own country and abroad (Bonn and Paris). It was thus that he was able to pursue a doctorate in the Arts Faculty of the Sorbonne (1970).

---

1. He was the guiding spirit of a journal addressed to young readers, *Skapanē* (Mattock), which was published from January 1961 to December 1963. On leaving *Skapanē*, he continued with a similar kind of journal, founding *Synoro* (Frontier), which came out from 1964 to 1967. The last issue (no. 41) although ready for publication, did not come out as a result of the colonels' *coup d'état* on 21 April 1967. See S. Zouboulakis, 'To "Synoro" kai ho Chrēstos Giannaras: Hē theologikē protasē tēs apoēthikopoiēsēs tou Christianismou' (*Synoro* and Christos Yannaras: The theological proposition of the de-ethicisation of Christianity), in *Anataraxeis stē metapolemikē theologia: Hē 'Theologia tou '60'*, pp. 315-26, here at p. 316.

He has spoken of this difficult phase in his life in an autobiographical work,[2] perhaps the best known of his books, entitled *Refuge of Ideas*. In this book he reveals the slow but decisive passage in his inner life from a moralistic Orthodoxy, devout and sentimental – 'pietistic' as he would later call it – and at the same time rationalistic and intellectually blinkered, to an Orthodoxy linked with freedom and grounded on the person and on the realisation of the truth of the person in Christ. This was the discovery of personalism as a fundamental structure of Orthodox anthropology, a discovery prompted by a Socratic figure, Dimitrios Koutroubis (1921-83).[3]

According to his own testimony this discovery of personalism began with the study of three authors:[4] Nicolas Berdyaev, little of whose work had been translated in the 1950s; the Swiss Christian psychiatrist, Paul Tournier (*Le personnage et la personne*, translated into Greek under the title *To prosōpeion kai hē prosōpikotēs*[5] [Mask and Personality]); and Igor Caruso's work, *Psychanalyse und Synthese der Existenz* (translated into Greek under the title *Psychanalysis kai synthesis tēs hyparxeōs*). The last two works came out in *Zōē*'s famous psychology series directed by the Greek psychiatrist, Aristotle A. Aspiotis (1910-83).[6] In his autobiographical work Yannaras claims that he was particularly struck by Paul Tournier:

> I absorbed Tournier's book by reading it over and over again. From his lines emerged something that seemed to me primarily true and substantial: the absolute priority of the human person

---

2. Christos Yannaras, *Kataphygion ideōn: Martyria* (Refuge of Ideas: Testimony) (Athens: Domos, 1987).
3. On the mythicisation of the role of Koutroubis, Zouboulakis makes some pertinent observations. See his '*To "Synoro" kai ho Chrēstos Giannaras*', pp. 316-17 and also p. 355 (response to objections).
4. None of the three authors is Greek. In the 1950s and early 1960s personalism actually played a very marginal role in the Greek world. Cf. Basilio Petrà, 'Personalist Thought in Greece in the Twentieth Century: A First Tentative Synthesis', *The Greek Orthodox Theological Review* 50, nos 1-4 (2005), pp. 2-48.
5. Yannaras, *Kataphygion ideōn*, pp. 257-58.
6. Aspiotis was for many years editor of the periodical *Aktines* (Rays), the organ of the Christian Union of Scientists, and was one of the major diffusers of the awareness of psychology as a liberal art in Greece in the twentieth century. He was the founder at the beginning of the 1950s of the Institute of Medical Psychology and Mental Hygiene in Athens and launched numerous series and separate publications to make the recent findings of the anthropological sciences known in Greece. Wishing to encourage an outgrowing of the prevailing mechanistic view of Man, he introduced the Greeks to texts of authors such as V. Frankl, H. Baruk, K. Schneider, L. Binswanger, P. Lersch, G. Allport, I. Caruso etc. In particular, he encouraged the development of the medicine of the person, under the guidance and with the collaboration of Paul Tournier.

not in an axiological or ideological sense, but a priority of life in relation to any schematisation of life – laws, values, moral codes – to any schematic mask which like the shirt of Nessus makes our real personhood disappear.[7]

The little he had read of Berdyaev was particularly revelatory. Through Berdyaev, Yannaras entered into a new world, into a new sense of the Christian faith. The page he devotes to describing Berdyaev's impact on his sense of Orthodoxy is illuminating:

> In the last years before I broke away, some readings had begun to open my eyes dimly to a different vision of life, to a sense of reality alien to that which had been imposed by my ideological militancy. Basically, I discovered Berdyaev. Few of his books had been translated into Greek at that time.[8] Yet they were enough to have had a revelatory effect on me. Here was a Christian author, and indeed an Orthodox one, who in his writings had not the slightest trace of the religiosity which I had known and which I was trying to live as the only authentic Christian life. He subjected moralism to a devastating critique, laid bare the narcissistic character of an individualistic religiosity, derided the turning of faith into a legalistic and ideological structure, had the audacity to respect the tragic adventure of atheism, and defended freedom as the absolute presupposition of a relationship with God.
>
> I was initiated by Berdyaev into my first sense of the difference between Eastern and Western Christianity. At university I had been taught the differences in dogma or the differences in administration and liturgical practice, but I had never suspected what realities of life were represented by these differences.
>
> I discovered with surprise that the elements of corruption and change in Christianity which Berdyaev noted in the Western tradition and stigmatised implacably were the same as those which I saw to be also dominant within the *Zōē* movement and to be tormenting our life: an egocentric self-sufficiency which was nourished by the turning of 'virtues' and of 'moral consistency' into idols. The substitution of experience by ideological 'certainty' – the priority of apologetics, or rational

---

7. Yannaras, *Kataphygion ideōn*, p. 258.
8. In fact, only one book had been translated by 1950, *The Destiny of Man*, under the title *Peri tou proorismou tou anthrōpou*. In 1952 Metropolitan Irenaeus of Samos translated *Spirit and Freedom*.

'proofs', the given 'authorities' for the reinforcement of truth. The schizophrenic dualism of body and soul, matter and spirit. The devaluation and depreciation of the sensible, the fear of love.[9]

So, it was through Berdyaev that Yannaras discovered a destiny common to a certain kind of Orthodoxy and the West, and at the same time gained a perception of what true Orthodoxy was. Even with all his peculiarity, Berdyaev put him into contact with certain themes of Russian diaspora theology which in the same period came to be set out by Koutroubis.

Passing through the hands of such masters, he then discovered the theology of Vladimir Lossky.[10] He rapidly absorbed his fundamental theses, in particular, his interpretation of the difference between the Eastern tradition and the Latin tradition. As early as June 1964 the *Kathēmerinē* newspaper published his article entitled '*Limos eperchomenos kai hē adraneia tōn syneidēseōn*' (The coming famine and the inertia of consciences),[11] in which Lossky's theses, assimilated via Olivier Clément, are well presented:

> By the light of this dogma [The Holy Trinity] Orthodoxy defines and describes the nature of Man. Man, created 'in the image' of the consubstantial (*homoousios*) and tripersonal God, is also himself *homoousios* by nature and *myriypostatos* in accordance with the persons (*prosōpa*). Every human being is a unique and unrepeatable *prosōpo*, but all these unique and unrepeatable persons are '*homoousia*' – of one and the same *ousia*. So only Man actualises his own hypostasis as *prosōpo*, when he finds himself in a communion of love with all the other persons.[12]

Later in 1966, in discussion with a Greek intellectual, Angelos Terzakis, in the journal *Epoches*, he explicitly takes up the Losskyan idea that the *prosōpo* is 'rationally indefinable and remains always unique, incomparable and "dissimilar"'.[13]

---

9. Yannaras, *Kataphygion ideōn*, pp. 256-57.
10. His celebrated *Essai sur la théologie de l'Église d'Orient* (1944) was published in Greek in Thessaloniki in 1964. Yannaras, however, already had some knowledge of Lossky's thinking.
11. The article was later reprinted in Christos Yannaras, *Timioi me tēn Orthodoxia: Neoellēnika theologika dokimia* (Honest with Orthodoxy: Modern Greek theological essays) (Athens: Astēr, 1968), pp. 17-22.
12. Christos Yannaras, '*Limos eperchomenos kai hē adraneia tōn syneidēseōn*', in idem, *Timioi me tēn Orthodoxia*, p. 21.
13. Christos Yannaras, '*Gia to problēma tou kakou*' (The problem of evil), in

This idea of Lossky's (in some form already present in Berdyaev) is based on the difference in Man between nature and person: the person indeed is for him irreducible to nature and nature is that which the person has in common with other human beings. Yannaras welcomes here such a thought and articulates some of his earliest moral reflections. Thus he defines evil as 'that which damages the human *prosōpo*, that which lays a snare for the *ousia* of his universal hypostasis, that which takes away the uniqueness and the "dissimilarity" of the *prosōpo*, the possibility of self determination, or, in other words, freedom of the *prosōpo* in the face of a uniform "nature"'.[14]

This discovery of personalism, as is apparent, is at the same time the discovery of a different Orthodoxy, an Orthodoxy which is also different from the West.

The idea quickly takes shape in this phase of Yannaras' thinking and becomes well established that Orthodoxy and the personal conception of Man go together precisely because – in Lossky's perspective – Orthodoxy generates the theological notion of the person and conversely the notion of the person finds in its theological source its clarification and the way in which it can be fully realised.

We are still dealing here with an early discovery, a youthful and enthusiastic discovery pervaded by an emotion intensified by the anguish of leaving *Zōē*. What is still lacking is analysis, an intellectual elaboration, and the exposition of the fecundity of this vision. Nevertheless, the fundamental horizon has been defined.

In this context the young Yannaras pays great attention to Russian literature and drinks deeply of Dostoevsky. It is from the great Russian writer that he arrives at a first unitary interpretation of the West and in relation to him a specific understanding of the mission of Orthodoxy.

2. Dostoevsky's Criticism of the West and the Mission of Orthodoxy

In 1964 when Yannaras departed for his studies in Europe and left *Zōē*, he was already bringing to maturity some of his ideas on the West and Orthodoxy's relationship to it. Through Dimitris Koutroubis (and Berdyaev) he had already come to know the theology of the diaspora. He had also developed contacts with Greek intellectuals such as Dimitris Pikionis and Zisimos Lorentzatos, the first of whom told him clearly that

---

Epoches, no. 34 (February 1966), pp. 115-19. The article was later reprinted in Yannaras, *Timioi me tēn Orthodoxia*, pp. 133-46, here at p. 135.
14. Ibid.

he had to leave *Zōē*.¹⁵ These were ideas forged largely through the literary work of Fyodor Dostoevsky (1821-81).¹⁶ The young Yannaras drew much from the great Russian writer in his rebellion against a Christianity that had been reduced to a matter of ethics. One of the Karamazov brothers, Alyosha, provided an ideal example for this,¹⁷ and for that reason he dedicated his earliest text to him in the collection published as *Timioi me tēn Orthodoxia* under the title, '*Peri* ēthikōn *protypōn (me anaphora ston Aliosa Karamazof)*' (Moral models [with reference to Alyosha Karamazov]).¹⁸

He also drew from him a precise interpretation of Western Christianity – the Christianity of Europe – and the conviction of the indispensability of Orthodoxy if Europe is going to find itself. He spoke

---

15. Yannaras, *Kataphygion ideōn*, pp. 275 ff., 300. It was to Lorentzatos that Yannaras dedicated *Timioi me tēn Orthodoxia*, his first collection of essays.
16. Yannaras wrote later on the role of Dostoevsky in his life: 'Dostoevsky has cut deeply into my life; he has been for me like the old man in the dream that Papadiamantis records' (Christos Yannaras, *Hē kokkinē plateia kai ho theios Arthouros* [Red Square and Uncle Arthur] [Athens: Domos, 1986], p. 35). This work is a kind of diary of his visit to Russia in May 1982 to take part in a Congress of Religions for Peace and against Nuclear Arms. He tried without success to be taken to Dostoevsky's grave.
17. Yannaras also attributes his theological vocation to the attraction of Alyosha's existential question: 'I know that I began to study theology – at the age of eighteen and while I was preparing for the Polytechnic up to the last moment – captivated by Alyosha Karamazov and by his choice without compromises: all or nothing. My family and teachers literally wept at my absurd choice. In those years to study theology was a public disgrace – in my case I concealed it from my relations' (Yannaras, *Hē kokkinē plateia*, p. 135).
18. Yannaras, *Timioi me tēn Orthodoxia*, pp. 92-97. This text was published in the November 1963 issue of the periodical already mentioned, *Skapanē*. On p. 96 he says, among other things, 'The essential content of faith, salvation by means of grace, the grafting of our corrupt nature into the new humanity of the New Adam, are realities that our contemporary social Christianity does not know and finds incomprehensible. We have pursued the social mission of Christianity with a culpable unilateralism, basing ourselves on the moral representation of the "integral [*artios*] human being", cultivating an overgrown superego and remaining blind to the true image of our fall and our corruption and to the necessity of God's grace.' Note that the idea of the *artios* human being relies on the words of 2 Timothy 3:17 and therefore has a biblical origin. Yannaras, nevertheless, severely criticises its purely ethical interpretation. Cf. a text of July 1964: '*Ho erchomenos: Schediasma mias charismatikēs parousias*' (He who comes: Outline of a charismatic advent), which was subsequently published in Yannaras, *Timioi me tēn Orthodoxia*, pp. 50-56, especially pp. 53-54. It should be mentioned that the ethical interpretation of *artios anthrōpos* was the ideal of one of the major figures of *Zōē*, namely A.A. Aspiotis (1910-83), on whom see p. 2, note 6 above.

of this in some length in a lecture which he gave in December 1965 and then published in instalments in the daily newspaper *Kathēmerinē* in February 1966:[19]

> For Dostoevsky Europe is not Christian. Catholicism has betrayed Christianity and transformed it into a worldly social programme. It has succumbed to Christ's third temptation, to a temptation of worldly power. The story of the Grand Inquisitor is the most radical criticism there is of Catholicism – the revelation of the religious dominion of the Antichrist – and this challenge has been left without a response by the Westerners. But for Dostoevsky even Protestantism has denied Christianity, has transformed it into a simple ethical system. Christ is only an ethical model to be imitated and therefore it is not important whether he is a mere man or both God and man. In Protestantism there is also room for the denial of the incarnation of the Word. Thus, for Dostoevsky nothing remains but Russia. Russia has Orthodoxy; it has the criteria for knowing the truth. Therefore, only in Russia can judgement exist. Europe does not have the possibility of acquiring a consciousness of judgement. It lacks the criteria because it relies upon an illusory Christianity; it believes it is Christian without being so.[20]

From Dostoevsky the young Yannaras also derived his perception of the responsibility towards the West. This is clearly apparent in some lucid pages that he published in *Kathēmerinē* on 18 March 1964 scarcely a month after leaving the *Zōē* theological brotherhood after ten years of militant activity (26 February).[21] The title of these articles is *Rōsikē kai hellēnikē orthodoxia* (Russian and Greek Orthodoxy).[22] Inspired by the *Speech on Pushkin* that Dostoevsky delivered on 8 June 1880,[23] and

---

19. Subsequently published in Yannaras *Timioi me tēn Orthodoxia*, pp. 155-77, under the title, '*Hē synantēsē Camus kai Ntostogiephski stous "Daimonismenous"*' (The meeting of Camus and Dostoevsky in *The Devils*).
20. Yannaras, *Timioi me tēn Orthodoxia*, pp. 155-56.
21. Cf. the bitter description of this moment in Yannaras, *Kataphygion ideōn*, pp. 342-43.
22. I read the text thus as reported by Yannaras, *Timioi me tēn Orthodoxia*, pp. 32-41. The text has been lightly revised with respect to its original publication in the newspaper.
23. On 2 May 1982 Yannaras had the opportunity to stop in front of the Pushkin monument in the square named after him in Moscow and recall the discourse pronounced by Dosteovsky: 'I stopped in front of it for a while, with emotion' (Yannaras, *Hē kokkinē plateia*, pp. 80-81).

particularly by some prophetic words contained in it – 'And later, I am fully confident, we, that is not me personally but those who will come after me, the Russians of the future, will all understand from the first till the last that to become a true Russian means precisely to aspire to the definitive reconciliation of the European contradictions'[24] – Yannaras speaks of the mission of Orthodoxy to save 'old Europe',[25] to give it new life. In saying this Yannaras seems to be in complete agreement with the vision of Georges Florovsky and the way he presents the first Slavophiles:

> The first Slavophiles had derived the idea of Russia's mission from European needs, from questions not yet resolved or unresolvable in the other half of the Christian world. It is to this feeling of Christian responsibility that the great justice and moral force of the early Slavophiles respond.[26]

Russian Orthodoxy, for Yannaras, has already in some way realised Dostoevsky's prophecy:

> A series of philosophers and theologians who one after another have played a central role in European life is the vital succession that the first group of Slavophiles has left as a legacy: Bulgakov, Florensky, Khomiakov, Berdyaev, and the contemporary Russian theology of the diaspora: Lossky, Florovsky, Evdokimov, Zander, Meyendorff, Schmemann are the spiritual presences immediately perceptible in European life. The second group make available to us today the responses of Orthodox theology to the contemporary Western man. With the first perception itself of the core of life that exists within the Russian Orthodox tradition, these men have in a marvellous way realised Dostoevsky's prophecy concerning the Russian national capacity for effecting a substantial reconciliation with the Western world.[27]

Yannaras insists – it should be noted – that nothing of the kind could have been realised if the Orthodox experience of ordinary people (the place of the conservation of the Orthodox truth) had not found flesh

---

24. Yannaras, *Timioi me tēn Orthodoxia*, p. 34.
25. Ibid., p. 33.
26. Cited from the Italian translation of Florovsky's *Ways of Russian Theology*, *Le vie della teologia russa* (Genoa: Marietti, 1987), p. 407. The Italian translation is only slightly different from the Greek one used by Yannaras.
27. Yannaras, *Timioi me tēn Orthodoxia*, pp. 33-34.

in the spiritual renewal of the Russian eighteenth century (St Seraphim of Sarov);[28] besides, the heirs of the first Slavophiles knew how to tone down the Slavophiles' exaggerations: the excessive emphasis on the popular element as if the people could take the place of the Fathers of the Church, 'the nationalism of Russian Orthodoxy, which has nourished the dreams and efforts of Panslavism.'[29]

An extraordinary symbol of this realisation of Dostoevsky's prophecy is for Yannaras the approach of Camus to *The Devils* and in general to the great Russian author in whom he recognises a prophetic character. Yannaras cites with emotion Camus' prologue to the French dramatised version of *The Devils*:

> For a long time Marx has been considered the prophet of the twentieth century. Today we know that what he prophesied is no longer what we expect. And we know very well that Dostoevsky was the true prophet. He prophesied the dominion of the Grand Inquisitor and the triumph of force over justice.... For me he is above all the writer who long before Nietzsche became aware of contemporary nihilism, who understood and foresaw its bestial and insane consequences and sought to establish the message of salvation.[30]

But there is something even more symbolic: Camus' intellectual journey brought him close to Orthodoxy. First of all, because he perceived the crisis of the West and wanted to go beyond Western illusions; secondly, because he was an atheist, which is to say he had rejected the gnoseological/rationalistic schemes of Western metaphysics (Aquinas, Descartes, the Enlightenment) in order to seek existential truth.[31] In Camus Yannaras saw an example of how a European, conscious of the death of God and touched by the experience of perdition, could be open to the Orthodox message

---

28. 'The roots of the Russian religious renaissance are hidden behind the line of intellectuals in the unknown *startsi* of the Church, in the mystical presences of living holiness, with the lived Orthodoxy of the authentically human and the authentically divine, which is the monasticism of the East. Clearly distinguishable among them is the most venerated St Seraphim of Sarov, who seems also to have been the prototype of Zosima in *Karamazov*' (Yannaras, *Timioi me tēn Orthodoxia*, pp. 35-36).
29. Yannaras, *Timioi me tēn Orthodoxia*, p. 36.
30. Ibid., p. 157.
31. Ibid., p. 156: 'In other words, truth is not a gnoseological problem but a matter of salvation. And this is a second reason why Camus is very close to Orthodoxy.'

of salvation, just as Dostoevsky had prophesied.³² In this connection Yannaras recalls a fact – told to him by Olivier Clément – that had struck him deeply:

> Albert Camus a little before his death read Lossky's book, *The Mystical Theology of the Eastern Church*. For Camus this theology was an unexpected surprise. 'This is something other,' he said, 'than what I am able to discuss.' And he began his dialogue with it by producing the dramatised version of Dostoevsky's *Devils*. But he did not do so in time to be able to continue.³³

For Yannaras, however, the true sign – a sign inaugurating a new epoch – that marked an opportunity in the West lay in the events of May 1968, in the widespread protests that erupted in the West at the end of the 1960s. Yannaras was to state this formally in his introduction to the first Greek edition of *The Freedom of Morality*:

> It seems that the time is right for Eastern Orthodox tradition to speak out. We are privileged perhaps to live in an historical period of a first exit from the scheme of a conventional morality which was sanctioned within the cultural confines of Europe by the Western deformation of Christianity – the morality that is based on the legal concept of sin, on the notion of individual transgression or individual merit, on the forensic concept of the relation of humanity to God.³⁴

And what about Greek Orthodoxy as it existed at that moment? For the young Yannaras Greek Orthodoxy was at a standstill; it was still in a situation similar to that which was experienced by Russian Orthodoxy at the beginning of the eighteenth century. That is to say, on the one hand, the institutional and cultural influence of the West, the forced Europeanisation that attempted and was still attempting to eradicate the Hellenism of the Orthodoxy actually experienced by the people,

---

32. Ibid., p. 172: 'Dostoevsky has shown, I think, with clarity that the response of Orthodoxy presupposes a crisis, a *perdition*. You must be "lost" in order to be "saved". . . . And Europe, in a continually growing measure, has the privilege of this perdition.'
33. Ibid.
34. Christos Yannaras, *Hē eleutheria tou ēthous: Dokimes gia mia orthodoxē theōrēsē tēs ethikēs* (The Freedom of morality: Essays towards an Orthodox vision of ethics) (Athens: Athēna, 1970), p. 10.

'of popular truth'³⁵ reduced to an archaeological exhibit; and, on the other hand, the popular radicalism of a few prophetic voices, the Greek Dostoevskies:

> Makriyannis, Solomos, Papadiamantis – it is clear that at least these have dug deep into the origins, not only into the lateral branches, but down into the roots. And these roots, which they have articulated prophetically like Dostoevsky, can nourish not only Greece but also the West which has grown old 'in the Sins' of rationalistic systems.³⁶

At a standstill in this situation, Greek Orthodoxy continued to live in a deep sleep while 'a real earthquake' was taking place, that is, the West's rediscovery of the Greek Fathers, of Byzantium, of Orthodoxy and even of the *Philokalia*.³⁷ Western theologians were publishing Eastern texts and studying them enthusiastically. The Greeks were limiting themselves to deriving benefits from tourism and feeling a certain Orthodox pride – nothing more than that.

Why did the same happen in Greece in the twentieth century as had happened in Russia in the nineteenth? Because the same miracle was necessary to create the spiritual presupposition: behind the Russian intellectuals was Seraphim of Sarov. Because in Greece too 'a handful of men' were bold enough to grasp 'the silence of action' or to put down roots in the 'soil of the Orthodox East' and offer today, a prophetic testimony about God, to give flesh to the *Logos* 'in silence, humility, abnegation and asceticism'.³⁸

However, where could such men be found and how could the temptation to identify Greek Orthodoxy simply with popular Greek culture or Green nationalism be avoided?

For Yannaras the prophetic capacity is historically represented by two figures: the monk and the martyr;³⁹ now, however – we are in 1964 – he must deal with martyrs capable of taking up the cross of technology⁴⁰ and with monks who are rediscovering the Orthodox sense of their

---

35. Yannaras, *Timioi me tēn Orthodoxia*, p. 38.
36. Ibid.
37. Ibid., pp. 38-39.
38. Ibid., p. 40.
39. Ibid., p. 51: 'The monk and the martyr embody the alert awareness of prophecy. They intervene in historical time to set a standard of historical duty (*chreos*). Their presence does not belong only to the past.'
40. Ibid., p. 54.

own mission.⁴¹ The capacity for prophecy is understood as the rejection of heretical Orthodoxy (the kind of Orthodoxy that in some way has accepted the two specific differences – the heresies – of the West: the rational foundation of faith and its reduction to moralistic pietism),⁴² of an Orthodoxy that is *anerastos*, that is, without *eros*, incapable of exhibiting the erotic substance of Christian experience,⁴³ and of an iconoclast orthodoxy (iconoclasm always accompanies a conservative pietism).⁴⁴

First of all, the prophetic capacity is understood as a Greek Orthodoxy that is capable of rediscovering its own ecumenical mission and can offer a vision of the universality of Orthodoxy,⁴⁵ avoiding reducing it to a form of nationalism, a problem peculiar to Greek Orthodoxy but also affecting Orthodoxy as a whole.⁴⁶

Is a renewal of this kind possible? Writing the preface to *Timioi me tēn Orthodoxia* (Honest with Orthodoxy) in Bonn in March 1967, Yannaras is pessimistic. He speaks of the end of Greek Orthodoxy, its end not as an institution but as a salvific presence:

---

41. Cf. the article '*Hairetikē Orthodoxia?*' (Heretical Orthodoxy?) which was published in 1966 and reprinted in Yannaras, *Timioi me tēn Orthodoxia*, pp. 59-73. On pp. 63-64 Yannaras says: 'The criterion of Orthodoxy is actual experience and the *mens* of the people – first of all experience. And because experience is first of all, it is monasticism that always has the first word in the self-awareness of Orthodoxy. But strictly speaking, monasticism is that which is lacking in Orthodoxy in Greece. It is lacking as a prophetic presence and as an eschatological witness to the life of the Church. . . . Today monasticism in the Greek state only preserves the consciousness of the past. Its witness has no rapport with experiential, theological certainties. . . . Today monasticism engages in journalism, raises its voice, anathematises – certainly not to testify to the Taboric experience of nature transfigured but to condemn the "moral crisis" or the antichrist papists who dare to cut their hair and their beard.'
42. Cf. ibid.
43. Cf. the article '*Erōs kai agamia: To drama henos anerastou Christianismou*' (Eros and celibacy: The drama of a loveless Christianity), first published in the spring of 1965 in *Synoro* and reprinted in Yannaras, *Timioi me tēn Orthodoxia*, pp. 74-83.
44. Cf. the article '*Eikonoklastes, hoi syntērētikoi tēs Orthodoxias*' (Iconoclasts, the conservatives of Orthodoxy), published in the winter of 1965 in *Synoro* and reprinted in Yannaras, *Timioi me tēn Orthodoxia*, pp. 84-91.
45. Cf. the article '*Helladikē kai oikoumenikē Orthodoxia*' (Helladic and ecumenical Orthodoxy), published in *Kathēmerinē* on 6 October 1964 and reprinted in Yannaras, *Timioi me tēn Orthodoxia*, pp. 42-49.
46. Cf. the article '*Hē apophasē De Oecumenismo tēs Deuterēs Batikanēs Synodou kai ho ethnikismos tēs Orthodoxias*' (The Decree *De Oecumenismo* of the Second Vatican Council and Orthodoxy's nationalism), published in the spring of 1966 in *Synoro* and reprinted in Yannaras, *Timioi me tēn Orthodoxia*, pp. 98-109.

a historical end does not necessarily always imply historical extinction; it can also mean historical aphasia. Orthodoxy in Greece does not show signs of a historical presence, but shows rather an absence, both in terms of theological self-consciousness – in dialogical relation with the present – and in terms of an updated worship, an ecclesial art and a contemporary monasticism and pastoral practice. The preservation of a museum-like tradition and an identification with the destinies of national life, even if objectively elements of survival, do not negate the fact of a historical end.[47]

Before concluding these reflections on what I have called the Dostoevskian phase of Yannaras' vision of the West, it seems useful to me to make two observations.

The first is this. The ecumenical aphasia of Greek Orthodoxy that Yannaras laments is already attributed to Western influence, even if for the time being this is seen principally as beginning with the Bavarian monarchy and is subsequently identified especially with the reduction of Christianity to pietism and moralism. This signifies that already at this time Greek Orthodoxy was aphasic because it was not truly Greek, because it was betraying its own Greek being. This same discourse on ecumenicity as the vocation of Greek Orthodoxy cannot help but appear ambiguous. If, on the one hand, it is true that a genuine Greek Orthodoxy is that which is open to ecumenicity (of which there are indications in Yannaras' texts of this period),[48] on the other hand, it can also be true that Greek Orthodoxy is truly ecumenical if it becomes more Greek, that is to say, more rooted in the Orthodox authenticity of the Greek Fathers, of Palamite hesychasm of popular Orthodox experience, of the Greek Dostoevskies. The first move leads to judging Hellenism in the light of ecumenicity and therefore to valuing the elements held in common with the West. The second, by contrast, leads to identifying ecumenicity with the *via aurea* of Orthodox Hellenism, in so far as it is Orthodox, that is, in so far as it is not Western: the real risk of this move is of transformation of anti-Westernism into a vital structural element of Yannaras' thought, as underlined by Pantelis Kalaitzidis, for whom the risk has become a reality. In fact, this second move seems not only to predominate but to be radicalised and to become much stronger as a result of what one might call the 'Heideggerian phase' in Yannaras' thought.

---

47. Ibid., p. 11.
48. Cf. the article '*Ho "laos tou Theou" ston Makrygiannē*' (The 'people of God' in Makriyannis), published in the fall of 1966 in *Synoro* and reprinted in Yannaras, *Timioi me tēn Orthodoxia*, pp. 178-90.

Here I would make my second observation. In 1966 the signs begin to emerge clearly of a reading by Yannaras of Heidegger's *Holzwege*.[49] Yannaras intuits that Heidegger's interpretation of nihilism, in the footsteps of Nietzsche, offers new elements with respect to Dostoevsky: it does not deal only with the rejection of the institutional deformation of Christianity (the Grand Inquisitor) and with the representation of nihilism as a Western crisis, as an experience of perdition which gives an opening to 'Orthodox' salvation;[50] under the heading of nihilism there is something more, something more radical which touches the very way in which human beings set about confronting being. Towards the end of 1966 Yannaras' ontological research takes off; he says it himself in the preface to *To prosōpo kai ho erōs* (Person and Eros).[51]

---

49. Cf. the article '*Scholio Orthodoxou ston "thanato tou Theou"*' (Comment of an Orthodox on the 'death of God'), published in the spring of 1966 in *Synoro* and reprinted in Yannaras, *Timioi me tēn Orthodoxia*, pp. 113-25. Yannaras cites Martin Heidegger, *Holzwege* (Frankfurt-am-Main: Klostermann, 1963). He dwells on the interpretation that Heidegger gives of nihilism in the footsteps of Nietzsche, anticipating some of his theses that will follow. It is not by chance that, with regard to the original text in *Synoro*, Yannaras adds a reference to his work of 1967 on Heidegger and the Areopagite, which we shall consider shortly.
50. The category of perdition is that which guides the first uses that Yannaras makes of Jean-Paul Sartre's thought, as appears in Yannaras, *Timioi me tēn Orthodoxia*, pp. 120-23, and in the reply given to A. Terzakis in *Epoches* of February 1966, '*Gia to problema tou kakou*' (The problem of evil), and reprinted in Yannaras, *Timioi me tēn Orthodoxia*, pp. 133-46.
51. I cite here from the publication of this work in *Deukalion* 3, no. 10 (1974), p. 145, where, in saying that its first version was his doctoral thesis in Thessaloniki, *To ontologikon periechomenon tēs theologikēs ennoias tou prosōpou* (The ontological content of the theological concept of the person) (Athens: Tip. Proodos, 1970), he adds: 'It was one of the stages or one of the phases of the attempt to study the themes that are brought together in the present work – in the midst of other pulses that have preceded and followed it, from the end of 1966, at about which time this attempt began, up to the present day.'

Chapter II
The Encounter with Heidegger and the Ontological Hermeneutic of the West: the Way of Apophaticism

1. Heidegger and the Nihilistic Outcome of Western Metaphysics: the Way beyond Nihilism; Eastern Apophaticism

'In Germany I learned a lot. How Western I was, how desperately Western.'[1]

However, Yannaras not only learned a lot of things in Germany; something further also happened: almost casually,[2] he says, he encountered Heidegger and Heidegger immediately lent him his style of writing:

> A marriage between poetic language and philosophy: that is what struck me in Heidegger. Precisely that which his suspicious Roman Catholic critics mocked. *Denken als Kunst, Mystik, Romantik*? [Thinking as art, or mysticism, or romanticism?] An ontology that refused to identify reality with its intellectual signification was incomprehensible to them. Their mocking suspicion justified his criticism, a criticism that demolished Western metaphysics.[3]

---

1. Christos Yannaras, *Ta kath' eauton* (Personal memories) (Athens: Ikaros, 1995), p. 48.
2. Ibid., p. 45.
3. Ibid., p. 47.

From that time Heidegger accompanied him on his journey: 'Heidegger was always close to me, a challenge of ontological realism.'[4] The encounter with Heidegger determined the ontological turn of Yannaras' thought, or his 'discovery' of ontology, and the closely linked ontological understanding of the West and also of Orthodoxy. One may rightly say – I believe – that in 1966 and thereafter the encounter with Heidegger remains the explicit/implicit horizon of Yannaras' reflection, in such a way that it becomes for him the canonically normative Heideggerian interpretation of the West.

By and large, in 1966 Yannaras confronts Heidegger in a thoughtful way, assimilating in a profound manner his ontological approach to reality and culture. He himself says that he wrote *Hē theologia tēs apousias kai tēs agnōsias tou Theou, me anaphores stis Areopagitikes syngraphes kai ston Martin Heidegger* (The theology of the absence and the ignorance of God, with reference to the Areopagitical writings and to Martin Heidegger) in Bonn between January 1966 and February 1967.[5] Later in 1967 he published this work in Athens.[6] Twenty years later, in publishing a revised version of the work, he was to say:

> It was my first essay to be published – the first little fruit up to that time of my study and research. The aim of my research was to clarify the differences between Greek philosophy and tradition and that of the West: differences that are not statically exhausted in the place (*topos*) of contemplation, but which determine the mode (*tropos*) or practice of life, that is to say, that which we call culture (*politismos*).[7]

---

4. Ibid., p. 50.
5. It is Yannaras himself who gives this date in a footnote to the last words of the book.
6. The book, which was printed in Athens at a private press, was then translated into French by J. Touraille: *De l'absence et de l'inconnaissance de Dieu d'après les écrits aréopagiques et Martin Heidegger*, Préface d'Olivier Clément (Paris: Cerf, 1971). This was the first of Yannaras' books to be translated into a Western language. The preface by Clément, 'Situation de la parole théologique selon la tradition orthodoxe', is really a complete essay occupying pp. 9-39 of the little volume (134 pages in all), to which are appended three pages of biographical information. On p. 41 Clément writes: 'From 1964 to 1967 Christos Yannaras studied in Germany. He discovered Heidegger's thinking and dwelt on it, sensing in the "death of God" the God of Western "onto-theology" (and the God of Androutsos, too!), the anticipation of the Inaccessible and the Crucified, of the Abyss and the Person ...'
7. Christos Yannaras, *Heidegger kai Areopagitēs: Hē theologia tēs apousias kai tēs agnōsias tou Theou* (Heidegger and the Areopagite: The theology of the

The fundamental idea that dominates this first work is in clear continuity with Heidegger; Western metaphysics, as it has developed ever since Plato, in order for its ontic interpretation of Being to prevail, has generated a historical process that – in relation to Being – both in its positive form (natural theology, rationalism) and in its negative form (Western apophaticism, irrationalism) leads – through Kant – to the Hegelian metaphysics of absolute subjectivity, and in the end 'transforms metaphysics into axiology'. In this light 'the reality of existents is no longer a logical necessity but an empirical or historical necessity' and 'the empirical or historical validity of existents is tied to their utility, not to their truth'.[8] Practical value becomes the criterion of the existents themselves in so far as they are existents. Yannaras underlines Heidegger's words in *Holzwege* where it is said that the death-blow to God, raised/reduced to the level of a supreme value, has not been inflicted by atheists but by the faithful and their theologians.[9] By his proclamation of the death of God Nietzsche has only made explicit the interior sense and necessity of the development of the mode of the Western approach to Being:

> It is evident that the proclamation of the 'death of God' sums up a historical process in the West both of natural theology and of apophaticism. Heidegger asserts that in Nietzsche's thought Christian theology is identified with Platonism and at the same time that: 'Christianity is for Nietzsche the historical, secular and political manifestation of the Church, and its demand for power within the framework of the formation of Western humanity.'[10]

---

absence and non-knowability of God), second revised edition (Athens: Domos, 1988), p. 9. The words are taken from the preface of the second edition, dated December 1986.

8. Yannaras, *De l'absence et de l'inconnaissance de Dieu*, p. 64.
9. Cf. Ibid., p. 65. The words are cited from Heidegger, *Holzwege* (1963 edition), pp. 239-40 (see *Heideggers Gesamtausgabe* 5, p. 260). Yannaras returns decisively to this idea, with reference to Heidegger's *Holzwege* and *Nietzsche*, in *Alētheia kai henotēta tēs Ekklēsias* (Truth and unity of the Church) (Athens: Grēgorē, 1977), p. 103: 'Heidegger has shown coherently that the "death of God" in the context of Western society has resulted from the "conceptualisation" (*Verbegrifflichung*) of religious experience, and thus it is the work of Western theology itself that has transformed the God of personal relation and communion into an abstract transcendental object of intellectual research and into an impersonal principle of moral authority.'
10. Yannaras quotes here from Heidegger's *Holzwege*, in particular from the essay: 'Nietzsche's words "God is dead"', in its French translation. He quotes from a passage in which Heidegger emphasises that institutional (ecclesiastical)

The Christian God is identified both with the intelligible world of classic metaphysics and with the cultural form of a social utility. Nietzsche's proclamation signifies the fundamental 'heresy' of Christianity in the West, the search for a rational and social form of intervention, the refutation of the paradox, that is, of the 'new' character, of the Church. The dogmatic, historical and canonical distinctions that separate Western Christianity from the original form of the Christian faith all contribute to this fundamental change in the way that the Church is conceived, which was the requirement for a temporal authority of the Church, thus surrendering to Christ's third temptation, as Dostoevsky had noted. The proclamation of the death of God is the historical result that passes a comprehensive judgement on the theological evolution of the West.[11]

What interests Yannaras in particular is the fact that for Heidegger the proclamation 'God is dead' does not at all signify the triumph of atheism but only that the place of God remains forever empty, because nothing can be said by human reason about His place without once again falling into ontological and axiological determinism:

> Heidegger goes so far as confidently to affirm that nihilism can have for a consequence both unbelief (in the sense of the idea of a falling away from Christian faith) and also Christianity itself. In other words, the two possible consequences of nihilism amount to the acceptance of either the absence or the unknowability of God.[12]

Heidegger then recognises that there is a space for apophaticism. However, as Yannaras notes, following Heidegger, it is a space closed by the West because: 'negation and affirmation are, in the Western metaphysical tradition, forms of critical discourse; they are "discursive

---

Christianity is not the same as the Christianity of the faith of the New Testament: 'Even a life that is not Christian can adhere to Christianity and use it as a power factor; just as, conversely, a Christian life does not necessarily have need of Christianity' (*Heidegger Gesamtausgabe* 5, p. 220). The connection between the will to power and Western religious institutions – present also in Dostoevsky – will frequently return in Yannaras; the distinction between New Testament faith and institution will also return.

11. Yannaras, *De l'absence et de l'inconnaissance de Dieu*, pp. 65-66. The idea of the Grand Inquisitor accompanies Yannaras' whole theological history; it is not by chance that it returns explicitly in the first pages of Yannaras' *Enantia stē thrēskeia* (Against religion) (Athens: Ikaros, 2006).
12. Yannaras, *De l'absence et de l'inconnaissance de Dieu*, p. 73. (There is also a reference here to *Holzwege*, p. 204.)

reasoning". Nothingness, as the result of negation, therefore has a rational provenance; it is a creation of the intellect, the most abstract of abstract conceptions.'¹³

There is, however, a different apophaticism – a non-Western one, and therefore one which remains outside the nihilistic necessity of Western metaphysics – which is the Eastern one, the apophaticism of Dionysius the Areopagite, as taken up by Vladimir Lossky and in some measure also by Nikos Nissiotis – who is mentioned at this point – the apophaticism that is grounded on the distinction between the essence and the energies of God. Yannaras emphasises that 'this distinction has been expressed in the whole of Greek patristic literature (Gregory of Nyssa, Basil the Great, Gregory the Theologian, Maximus the Confessor, John Damascene, and Gregory Palamas)' and that 'it reveals the specific difference that differentiates Eastern apophaticism from its Western version'.¹⁴

What Yannaras is discussing is an apophaticism characterised by the renunciation of the claim to attain knowledge of God in the discursive manner of rational affirmations and negations:

> It is evident [says Yannaras] that the apophatic position can not be identified with the theology of negations. Historically this identification is realised in Western apophaticism. It presupposes natural affirmative knowledge and at the same time its negation, that is to say, the relinquishing of the objective authority of sensible symbols. The apophatic position is not just a further method, even if a more effective one for acquiring natural knowledge of God, but a way that coincides with the affirmation of the human person, that is to say, which defines a universal position towards truth, a gesture of freedom with regard to the sufficiency of rational definitions. The relinquishing is here a voluntary liberation from the arbitrary nature of reason. It signifies the affirmation of a new dimension of knowledge that is defined by the person's capacity for dialogue.¹⁵

In so far as it is 'a renunciation of every conceptual necessity' and 'a negation of conceptual idols of God',¹⁶ this theological apophaticism seems to coincide objectively with Heideggerian nihilism: 'By its respect for the limits of sceptical thought and its testimony to the inability of thought to

---

13. Ibid.
14. Ibid., p. 99.
15. Ibid., pp. 87-88.
16. Ibid., p. 93.

go beyond ontological and axiological definitions, Heidegger's nihilism seems to fit well with that which here, on the basis of the Areopagitical writings, we have called "renunciation'":[17]

> Indeed, in the teaching of the Areopagite, beings have no reference to the divine essence. It is for this reason that knowledge of God is impossible on the basis of the analogy of being. A definition, of whatever kind, of the essence of beings originating in the ideas or the existential causes in the Being of God would make the created world a defective reflection of the divine essence, as Platonism would have it. In the Areopagitical writings beings are defined as the result not of the essence but of the will of God.[18]

This Areopagitical vision, both in the renunciation that it connotes and in its distinction between essence and energies does not condemn Man to the non-knowledge of God; on the contrary, it opens up the possibility of a knowledge that goes beyond conceptual determinations:

> The divine energies – the ineffable possibility that the divine essence, which is unknown, imparticipable and incommunicable, has of being offered as a will for personal communion – are the foundation of apophatic 'knowledge'. The abyss of the 'natural' distance of beings from God (the theological Nothingness that is inexpressible 'outside' the divine essence) is covered and bridged by the divine energies, thanks to which God becomes accessible under certain conditions, yet at the same time remains perfectly inaccessible.[19]

Personal communion is the way that preserves the truth of apophaticism and at the same time makes possible the truth of knowledge: 'apophatic knowledge is the result of personal communion between Man and God, of the "participation" of Man in the Godhead as a whole. The divine energies elicit an experience of participation in the imparticipable Godhead and this experience constitutes the sole possibility of knowing God.'[20] God is known through the 'ecstatic communion between God and Man',[21] which is brought about for the first time in a radical manner in the incarnation of God in Man and has rendered possible for all the deification of the human person:

---

17. Ibid., p. 88.
18. Ibid., p. 99.
19. Ibid., p. 103.
20. Ibid., p. 105.
21. Ibid., p. 120.

> It is clear [Yannaras formally declares] that what we have called apophatic knowledge is ultimately identified with the deification of the human person. It is 'the vision and the cognisance' and the 'divine participation' in God, the loving communion with Him that becomes possible through the divine energies.[22]

Eastern apophaticism thus goes beyond Heidegger in that it opens the way to an ontology of the person. If in this first essay of 1967 Yannaras does not go so far as to use this technical language in a formal sense, he clearly does so twenty years later when he writes in a new edition of the work:

> The nihilism of Heidegger, as respect for the unrestricted limits of questioning thought – as refusal to subject God and Being to conceptual constructs – seems provisionally to fit in with what we have here called, in reliance on the Areopagitical writings, apophatic renunciation. It differs crucially from the apophaticism of the Areopagite both in its presuppositions and in its consequences, presuppositions and consequences that make up the ontology of the person, the linking of apophaticism to the existential principle of freedom and otherness.[23]

2. Yannaras' 'Conversion to Ontology' and the Discovery of the Ontological Difference with the West: the Rediscovery of 'Greek Metaphysics' and Its Connection with Apophaticism

The outline of the 1967 essay reveals the decisive importance of the discovery of Heidegger in the thinking of the young Yannaras: what it concerns is a real 'conversion to ontology'.

I use this term because it seems to me the most appropriate for indicating the profundity and seriousness of what happened to Yannaras: he took up the ontological approach as the normal way of approaching questions concerning Man and his existence; he appropriates in a particular way the ontological hermeneutics which Heidegger applies to Western history and intuits in it the way forward to a fascinating possibility of rethinking the history of the Orthodox East itself and in particular of (Orthodox) Hellenism.

This describes a decisive transition, the importance of which the author himself underlines when in the mid-1990s he reassesses the

---
22. Ibid.
23. Ibid., p. 89 (Eng trans. Ventis).

evolution of his thinking in an autobiographical passage. In a most lucid manner he reveals the significance which this discovery of Heideggerian ontology had for him and shows how in him – in so far as he was a Greek intellectual – there arose from it an intellectual vocation, the prospect of a true and personal programme of work that he was to develop in a consistent manner in the years to come:

> The study of ontology shed light on the evolution of culture in Europe, its necessary conclusion in nihilism – an evolution and conclusion which Nietzsche had deciphered at an opportune moment and Heidegger had exploited. The illumination of the historical process is moreover for a Greek scholar the most fertile challenge to self-awareness which he could encounter. How and why the ancient Greek theory of knowledge – the identification of *alētheuein* with *koinōnein*[24] – preserves the ontology of the ancient Greeks centred on *ousia* from ending up in nihilism. How and why a new ontology of Christian experience espouses the flesh of Greek reason (*logos*) and remains the same theory of knowledge despite the ontological reversal, proving its organic continuity with the Greek philosophical struggle with the ontological question. How, when and why medieval Europe's break with the Greek tradition, the radical reversal of the terms of Greek culture, on the level both of the theory of knowledge and ontology, both took place and what it consists in. How there emerges from the epistemological demand for individualistic intellectual certainty the phenomenon of a dogmatic ideology which leads, for the first time in history, to the monstrous formation of totalitarianism. In what degree the person-centred ontological realism of the Byzantines can function today as a proposal for escaping from the nihilistic impasse – how it can be articulated in the language of today's debates, how it can be in dialogue with Heidegger and

---

24. The translation of these Greek words, in so far as the first is concerned, is not particularly difficult. The principal difficulty concerns the second, because *koinōnia* and *koinōnein* may be translated either in terms of sociality or in terms of communality. Yannaras emphasises in all his thinking that the authentic Greek sense tends more towards communality. See a very precise statement of this in *Exi philosophikes zōgraphies: 'Ekomisa eis tēn Technēn'* (Six philosophical pictures: 'I have brought to Art') (Athens: Ikaros, 2011), p. 42: 'At that time the *koinōniko* fact (the dynamic becoming of the relations of *koinōnia*) was alienated into *societas*: "an association for a common interest". For this reason, in cases where Yannaras uses the Greek sense as he perceives it, I shall use the terms communion, communal etc.

Sartre, with the theatre of the absurd, with the surrealism of art and poetry, with the principles of political economy, or with the language of quantum mechanics.[25]

This passage is probably the clearest and most forceful exposition of the truth of the fact just noted: the whole of Yannaras' intellectual research flows rigorously from the encounter with Heidegger (with his ontology) and from an intuitive insight that he suddenly had of the possibilities of thinking and reflection that the perspectives opened up by Heidegger offered to a Greek Orthodox intellectual. The ontological encounter with Heidegger – and to some extent with Sartre, 'the most important theologian in the Western philosophical tradition'[26] – was

25. Yannaras, *Ta kath' eauton*, pp. 74-75.
26. Yannaras pays particular attention to the thought of Jean-Paul Sartre, as he shows in *Schediasma eisagōgēs stē philosophia* (An outline introduction to philosophy) (Athens: Domos, 1981), second edition 1988. On pp. 139-41 (pp. 282-83 of the second edition) he explains his reasons as follows: 'Despite Sartre's global reputation (greater indeed than that experienced by any other philosopher in his own lifetime), I would venture to say that the most important aspect of his philosophical contribution to the investigation of the ontological question remains largely unknown. And I would summarise this contribution in the assertion that for the first time in the history of Western European philosophy the ontological problem rediscovers in Sartre the radical quality of the Greek theological debate. However paradoxical it may seem, Sartre's ontological views represent for Western philosophy its highest theological moment – Sartre is without doubt the most important theologian in the West's philosophical tradition. Why do I attribute a theological dimension to Sartre's work and indeed view it as the most important aspect of his philosophy? Because only he brings the ontological problem back to its theological starting point, that is, to the question about the given or otherwise character of existence, about the identification of the existential principle of being with either freedom or necessity. . . . For Sartre the problem of God (as formerly also for Greek philosophy of the early and middle Christian periods) is judged fundamentally by the question of a given or otherwise character of existential otherness – that is, it is judged by the ontological content of freedom: either freedom constitutes Being as an event of communion and self-transcendence, and consequently as existential otherness (in which case only the triadicity of God responds to the problem of the hypostatic principle of Being), or freedom is the given and uninterrupted mode of the existential otherness of the subject, in which case its realisation necessarily nullifies Being as essence or nature (and then the existence of God is absolutely contradictory' (Eng. trans., Christos Yannaras, *The Schism in Philosophy: The Hellenic Perspective and its Western Reversal* [Brookline, MA: Holy Cross Orthodox Press, 2015], pp. 248-49). In *Orthos logos kai koinōnikē praktikē* (Correct reason and social practice) (Athens: Domos, 1984), p. 93, Yannaras goes on to speak of 'Sartre's reverse theology'.

to remain a kind of permanent *Leitmotiv* of his thinking. Some of his texts, even recent ones, demonstrate that for him Heidegger's nihilistic ontology is the last word in Western ontology: only a personalist Greek ontology offers a true alternative.[27] The passage just cited is highly significant: in it, Yannaras himself offers a unified interpretation of all his activity after 1967, beginning with his discovery of Heidegger's ontological hermeneutics.

The list of lines of research that he draws up in this passage is almost complete. Here we can only give the reader a taste of them by mentioning a few, indispensable for our exposition, without establishing a hierarchy among them because they are all tightly interwoven.

In the first place, there is the claim of a continuity on the level of gnoseology, a continuity that endures despite from Antiquity to Christianity with the ontological reversal that such a transition entails. The claim carries with it the need for a Greek rereading of ancient Greek philosophy, an idea that is itself based on Heidegger:[28] it appears to him

---

27. This conviction remains a fixed point in Yannaras' thinking: 'At any rate, observing the terms or criteria of methodological coherence, of respect for the limits of language, of an alert awareness regarding the difference between signifiers and what is signified, of a frank insistence on the primacy of experience and not of the intellect (with all its presuppositions), I think – a personal opinion – that historically only two ontological visions may claim a certain completeness: the person-centred ontology of ecclesial apophatism (which today we call 'Byzantine') and the nihilistic ontology of Martin Heidegger' (Christos Yannaras, *Kommatokratia: Otan hoi polites hyperpsēphizoun tē leēlasia tēs zōēs tous* [Partyocracy: When citizens vote in favour of the plundering of their life] [Athens: Patakē, 2002], p. 238); 'One might venture, although not without risk of arbitrariness (a risk that accompanies any inferential generalisation), to make an axiological judgement (subject, like any general hermeneutic proposition, to verification or falsification) that the more coherent rational and empirical systematic responses that have been made up to now to the ontological problem may be reduced to two: the nihilistic ontology of Martin Heidegger and the personalist ontology of the Christian ecclesial tradition. These are methodologically the most satisfactory' (Christos Yannaras, *To ainigma tou kakou* [The enigma of evil] [Athens: Ikaros, 2008], p. 244; Eng. trans., Christos Yannaras, *The Enigma of Evil* [Brookline, MA: Holy Cross Orthodox Press, 2012], p. 129).
28. It has been noted that for Heidegger the Latin translation of the Greek terms is in reality a translation into a different mode of thinking about the experience of being and it is precisely with this translation that the lowering of the ground begins in Western thought, as he says himself. This theme is prominent in 'Der Ursprung des Kunstwerkes', the first essay collected in *Holzwege* (*Heidegger Gesamtausgabe* 5, pp. 7-8). Yannaras underlines this new Heideggerian way of reading Plato and Aristotle in the preface of *To prosōpo kai ho erōs* from the first edition onwards.

an especially urgent task to reread Aristotle's philosophy which has been deformed by the scholastic and Western European understanding of it.[29] The Christian reversal of ontology, well expressed by the theology of the Cappadocians according to the interpretation of John Zizioulas,[30]

---

29. Christos Yannaras in *Schediasma eisagōgēs stē philosophia*, vol. 2, pp. 15 and 41, distinguishes two senses of being in the history of Western philosophy, the ontic (with the basic question: 'What is it that makes being be?') and the ontological (with the basic question: 'What is the difference between being and beings?') (Cf. Yannaras, *The Schism in Philosophy*, pp. 165-93.) The ontic version goes back to Aristotle, whereas the ontological finds 'its first coherent configuration' (p. 40) in Heidegger. The first underlies Heidegger's critique and leads to a nihilistic result; the second reduces ontology to gnoseology (arriving at an individualist agnosticism). Citing Heidegger's *Über den Humanismus*, he writes: 'Truth is of interest as a definition of the limits of thought in so far as it is thought; ontology is identified with the theory of knowledge' (p. 53). Nevertheless, Yannaras discusses the Aristotelian authenticity of the ontic concept; his own view is rather that Aristotle lies at the origin of both concepts: 'All the presuppositions exist for maintaining that from his texts can be derived both the ontic concept and the ontological concept of being: his discussions have permitted both of these approaches to the ontological problem' (p. 29).
30. There is an enthusiastic article in the newspaper *To Bēma* (Tribune) of 9 July 1977, entitled '*Enas logos prin apo tēn koinē agora*' (A word before the common market), in which he presents the recently published – in 1977 – essay of John Zizioulas, '*Apo to prosōpeion eis to prosōpon*' (From the mask to the person), on which see Basilio Petrà, '*Zēzioulas, Iōannēs*', in A. Pavan (ed), *Enciclopedia della persona nel xx secolo* (Naples: Edizioni Scientifiche Italiane, 2008), pp. 1142-47. Cf. now another article in Christos Yannaras, *Hē neoellēnikē tautotēta* (Modern Greek identity) (Athens: Grēgorē, 1978), pp. 93-101. Yannaras makes ample reference to the theses of John Zizioulas in the 1981 edition of *Schediasma eisagōgēs stē philosophia*, vol. 2, pp. 54-80, insisting on the ontological significance of the difference between the West's vision of the Trinity and that of the East: 'When the Church speaks of the unicity of God, of a God who is one and at the same time threefold, it does not refer the unity to the ontological priority of the *Ousia* but to the principle or ontological cause of the personal-trinitarian life of God who is one Person, the Person of God-Father. The personal existence of God (the Father) constitutes, makes the hypostasis of His *Ousia*, that is, His Being: freely and through love He generates the Son and makes the Holy Spirit to proceed. The ontological principle of the otherness and personal freedom of God refers not to an *essential* (*ousiastikē*) possibility in itself, but to the fact that God is Father, that He generates and causes to proceed the Son and the Spirit. That which God is, is established by the personal freedom of the Father, and exists (becomes a hypostasis) as an event of freedom, that is, of communion of personal hypostasis. When Christian revelation defines that "God is love" (1 John 4:16), it refers not to a particular property of God's "behaviour" but to that which God *is* as "the fullness of personal trinitarian communion"' (p. 75). He does not miss the opportunity, however, of noting that his volume *Person and Eros*, which we

with his affirmation of the identity of person (*prosōpo*) and hypostasis,[31] does not affect the essential aspect of this continuity. Yannaras says it in numerous texts, in a challenging manner;[32] he came to speak in this sense of a Greek metaphysics (*Hē hellēnikē metaphysikē*):

> Both in ancient Greece and in the Christianised Greece that followed the criterion for the verification of knowledge was communally centred (*koinōniokentriko*). A proposition is true not when it corresponds to the external rules of a codified method or an infallible authority, but when it coincides (*sym-ballei*) (goes together with, agrees with) the experience of all – when all share the same opinion and each brings a testimony (Democritus). The Greeks, with Aristotle at their head, were the first to give shape to the rational method or formal logic but they never substituted the individual intellectual certainty of correct syllogistic reasoning for the priority of shared (*koinōnoumenē*) experience. The rational method (*to orthōs dianoeisthai*) always and exclusively has facilitated access to participation in truth (*to orthōs koinōnein*).[33]

Yannaras was to see in this continuity the permanent source of Greek cultural identity, of the universal mission of Hellenism, which has always been called upon to delineate the authentically human mode of

---

shall examine, is chronologically the first attempt to present a systematic account of the ontology of the Greek Fathers and discuss its relationship to the later ontological debate' (Yannaras, *The Schism in Philosophy*, 199, n. 6).

31. 'But if the person (*prosōpo*) is the hypostasis of Being, then its existence is not an ontological given but a dynamic "realisation" (*katorthōma*). Thus, the person is a mode of existence that is brought about as freedom, freedom from every necessity, from every limit, freedom from the limitation of death. The survival of personal otherness beyond death is not guaranteed as some property of essence or nature like the "immortality of the soul", because in that case it is a forced immortality that dissolves the person. The person transcends death because it itself constitutes the hypostasis of existence as life, as "eternal life". And life is the communion of persons; it is love, that ontological event that constitutes even the unique definition of God (1 John 4:8)' (Yannaras, *Hē Neoellēnikē tautotēta*, pp. 99-100).

32. In Christos Yannaras, *Orthodoxia kai Dysē: Hē theologia stēn Hellada sēmera* (Orthodoxy and the West: theology in Greece today) (Athens: Domos, 1972), p. 136, he writes: 'And it is impossible to arrive at the true Plato and Aristotle, without the Byzantine Fathers and the *Synaxary* of the Tourkokratia and the mystagogic profundity of the Orthodox icon.'

33. Christos Yannaras, *Politistikē diplōmatia: Protheōria hellēnikou schediasmou* (Cultural diplomacy: A preliminary review of a Greek project] (Athens: Ikaros, 2001), p. 95.

existence: he states it very succinctly in a piece welcoming the essay by Zizioulas which has already been mentioned.³⁴ I would note in passing that Yannaras sees in Zizioulas' theses a substantial confirmation of his own ontological perspectives which from the beginning establish an essential connection between personal existence, relationship, freedom, love and truth:

> Consequently, personal existence, existence as relation, relation as freedom of love is the mode of that which truly (*ontōs*) exists, namely truth. Free from any existential subjection to the principle (*logos*) of his essence or nature, God can exist also by assuming human nature, as the God-man Jesus, transmitting also to Man the possibility of existing free from the existential limitations of his nature, in the mode of that which really exists, namely, love.³⁵

These words allow us to perceive the near-inevitability of the second line of investigation, namely, the claim of Greek (Byzantine) ontology – personalist and apophatic with the category of relation at its centre (*schesē*)³⁶ – as the way out of the West's nihilistic impasse. Yannaras

---

34. 'I believe [he says] that among the large scholarly output of studies that are insignificant and imitative of what is produced in the West, one can nevertheless discern a certain number that prepare the way for the articulation of a contemporary word with a Greek identity and with consequences that are vital for the universal human journey. For today a word that is essentially Greek must signify the recapitulation of the Greek diachronic unity and identity not in theses or abstract opinions, but in the determination of a mode of existence for humanity and, consequently, of a historical and social realisation that differentiates itself radically from the nightmare without an exit of Western culture (and its philosophical and theological presuppositions), of the culture of the alienation and neutralisation of humanity within the boundaries of a utilitarian positivism of knowledge. To articulate a word of this kind, beyond empty arrogant claims and rhetorical traditionalism, would signify first of all that it assumes as its meaning and goal the historical survival of the modern Greeks, that is to say, that the hope exists that our unclear and inconsistent state objectives, our educational system and our foreign policy should acquire flesh. It would signify that Greekness (*Hellēnismos*) should become again an event with important consequences for human history as a whole, for the universal liberation of human beings from the inhumanity of 'objective' solutions and of the positivism of "programmes for happiness"' (Yannaras, *Hē Noellēnikē tautotēta*, pp. 94-95).
35. Yannaras, *Politistikē Diplōmatia*, pp. 93-94.
36. The first and most consistent publication in this direction was *To prosōpo kai ho erōs*, a work already cited and which preceded even Zizioulas's essay. The centrality of the category of relation was to become formal and direct in *Ontologia tēs schesēs* (Ontology of relation) (Athens: Ikaros, 2004).

seems motivated by the conviction of a historical mission: to manifest the salvific and veridical fecundity of Greek (Orthodox) ontology. From this comes his determined engagement with the attempt to demonstrate this by criticising the signs of the Western deformation of ontology in contemporary terms – in various fields of human existence of culture – and at the same time putting this conviction to the proof of today's knowledge. If the encounter begins with Heidegger, Sartre, political economy and quantum mechanics, it was to continue thereafter with linguistics, jurisprudence, postmodernism, psychology and neurobiology; the dialogue and encounter become intense and lively with thinkers such as Karl Marx, Max Weber, Karl Popper, Jacques Lacan, Ludwig Wittgenstein etc., in the attempt to respond in an ontologically coherent manner to fundamental questions such as those concerning the truth of God, eros, beauty, evil and death.

The critique of the Western deformation of ontology, the inevitable consequence of a gnoseological approach that is not authentically apophatic, is necessary, or rather, is the first necessity.[37]

Without this mode of Western existence, which also altered the reception of Greek philosophy that began the path towards nihilism, the Greek reception of the Christian message – the Orthodox one – would have maintained its authentic path. However, that is not how it happened. The West constructed a Christianity in accordance with the Western approach to ontology; the schism of 1054 was not simply a separation on the levels of dogma and discipline; it was an ontological schism.[38]

---

37. This has led some to maintain that the anti-westernism in Yannaras' thought has a structural character. See P. Kalaitzidis, 'Hellēnikotēta kai antidytikismos stē "Theologia tou '60"' (Greekness and anti-westernism in the 'Theology of the 1960s'), doctoral dissertation, Department of Theology, Aristotle University of Thessaloniki, 2008, esp. pp. 209-584; idem, 'Hē anakalypsē tēs hellēnikotētas kai ho theologikos antidykitismos', in P. Kalaitzidis, Th.N. Papathanasiou and Th. Ampatzidis (eds), *Anataraxeis stē metapolemikē theologia* (Athens: Indiktos, 2009), pp. 429-514, esp. pp. 479-514.
38. On this subject the interview given by Yannaras to Michel Stavrou and reported in Greek in Christos Yannaras, *Mia synenteuxē* (An interview) in *Synaxē* 34 (1990), pp. 69-78, is of great interest. Yannaras increasingly comes to accept the idea that the schism has its roots in the Augustinian approach to gnoseology and ontology and in the assumption of a hegemonic role in the West by the Germanic tribes, especially the Franks, a thesis particularly dear to J.S. Romanides. Cf. in particular Christos Yannaras, '*To Schisma hōs politistikē rogmē tēs Eurōpēs*' (The Schism as a cultural fracture of Europe), in idem, *Kommatokratia*, pp. 119-39. This is the text of the controversial lecture given in 2000 at the Fondazione Giovanni Agnelli of Turin, Italy. A sharp confrontation with Hervé Legrand took place there.

The excommunication on the part of the Eastern Church was an act of charity in the hope of the salvation of humankind.[39] Already in 1970 Yannaras lists the Western errors that are fundamental to the Western mode of thinking/living Christianity. He lists these errors in a lecture he gave in Boston entitled 'Orthodoxy and the West':[40]

> Let us summarise the basic elements of the stance of Western man in the face of the world and history. These are the following: the priority of the conceptual explication of revealed truth; the dividing boundary between the transcendent and the worldly; the will to dominate nature and history; the 'banishment' of God to an empirically unreachable realm; the separation of religion from life and the reduction of religion to symbols; the elimination of ontology, that is to say, dogma, and its substitution by ethics.[41]

The list is incomplete. It was subsequently enriched and certain changes became central: individualism, legalism, authoritarianism, utilitarianism, totalitarianism etc.

The critique of the West, as has often been said and as it appears here, is therefore an ontological critique. Certainly, it has a reference that is also geographical but only in so far as it is a place marked in an exemplary fashion by a mode of existence – an *ethos* – that has precise ontological connotations. The critique of the West can therefore become a critique of that which is 'Western' wherever it manifests itself. Yannaras regards the critique of the West as particularly urgent where it lies hidden within Orthodoxy *par excellence*, the Orthodoxy of the Greeks. Yannaras' scathing attacks on the West in Greece are well known; academic theology does not escape his lash, nor does the pietism of the theological brotherhoods, nor does even Athonite monasticism (in particular, Nikodemos the Hagiorite), nor do even the Sacred Canons.[42]

---

39. Cf. Christos Yannaras, *Alētheia kai henotēta tēs Ekklēsias* (Athens: Grēgorē, 1977), p. 148.
40. This was to be published under the same title in A.J. Philippou (ed), *Orthodoxy, Life and Freedom: Essays in Honour of Archbishop Iakovos* (Oxford: Studion Publications, 1973), pp. 130-47. The Greek text was published a little later together with another essay, 'La théologie en Grèce aujourd'hui', previously published in French, in *Orthodoxia kai Dysē: Hē theologia stēn Hellada sēmera*.
41. Yannaras, 'Orthodoxy and the West', pp. 134-35.
42. The first work in which these attacks are evident in a harsh but very interesting manner is *Hē eleutheria tou ēthous* (The freedom of morality). The first edition of this work – as already noted – bore the subtitle: *Dokimes gia mia orthodoxē theōrēsē tēs ēthikēs* (Attempts at an Orthodox vision of ethics). Following strong

Within the critique of the West the emergence and imposition of a term may be noted by which Yannaras synthesises and defines the essential deformation that the Western ontological approach inflicts on the gospel message and the ecclesial event. This is the term *thrēskeiopoiēsē* ('religionisation') which indicates the religious institutionalisation or the transformation of the gospel event into a religion. This is a term we shall return to later.

3. Eastern Apophaticism and Orthodox Apologetics: the Gnoseological Topicality of Apophaticism and Its Iconological Character

The gnoseological importance of apophaticism in its Eastern form is at the centre of a brief but important essay that Yannaras published in the mid-1970s dealing with the question of apologetics in the context of Orthodox theology. His intention is not so much to expound the Eastern apologetic tradition; he wishes rather to establish what path an authentic Orthodox apologetics can take. His point of departure, not by chance, is a criticism of Greek academic apologetics influenced by the Western model, or by that which he calls 'the secularisation of apologetics' and which is a particular symptom of the more general phenomenon of 'the alienation of theological gnoseology' that had begun in the West already 'in the twelfth century and had transformed theology into a "science", subject to the aims and principles (*regulae, axiomata, principia*) of rational coherence and historical accuracy'.[43] It is an aspect of this rationalism that can only end up in nihilism, in the 'death of God'. Yannaras underlines this by citing Heidegger and the *Holzwege*:[44]

> Even if one may concede that academic apologetics has the merit of having tried to answer a culture that is positivistic and anti-religious by using its own methods, nevertheless a true Orthodox apologetics can be initiated solely by adequately distinguishing

---

reactions against it, Yannaras prepared a second and notably revised edition, published in Athens by Grēgorē in 1979, without the subtitle. A third edition, revised in a very limited manner in comparison with the second edition, was published in Athens by Ikaros in 2002. The most complete attempt to give a systematic critique of the West's influence in Greece is, of course, Christos Yannaras, *Orthodoxia kai Dysē stē neōterē Hellada* (Orthodoxy and the West in modern Greece) (Athens: Domos, 1992).

43. *Hē apologētikē sta horia tēs orthodoxou theologias* (Apologetics in the context of Orthodox theology) (Athens: Grēgorē, 1975), p. 13.
44. Ibid., p. 17, n. l.

various 'levels of knowledge'. One must distinguish between 'the dynamic-apophatic knowledge of Christian theology' and 'the positivistic knowledge of empirical utilitarianism'.[45] If the God of the Church is not an object of the intellect or the senses that is subject to the verification of scientific observation or rational analysis but is a Person who reveals himself within the context of a personal relationship (in the immediacy of loving communion or through the acceptance and full awareness of his personal energies), then the way of the knowledge of God can not be the same way as that which leads to the knowledge of the objects of science. In the theological tradition of the Eastern Church the problem of the knowledge of God (but also of Man and the cosmos) is not expressed as a need for intellectual-objective definitions, nor is it exhausted as a reply to the coincidence of the concept with the object conceived; it is an experiential and moral challenge to bring personal existence back to truth 'in accordance with nature' and this truth finds in intellectual formulations simply the outer forms or terms that protect it. Personal knowledge presupposes the existential-personal integrity of Man, the unity of the intellect and the heart, of *logos* and action, of *ethos* and being, a unity that assures the universal immediacy and experiential demonstrability of 'true knowledge'. And the tragic error of rationalistic apologetics is that it has subjected this universality and this dynamics of theological truth to the conventional schemes of logical necessity.[46]

This distinction between levels of cognition has been lost in Western rationalism. Nevertheless, it has been preserved in some degree and for the most part is again making its appearance. To judge from what Yannaras says, one can speak of a kind of vogue for apophaticism in the West:

A phenomenon such as art, in the context of Western society, has managed to safeguard the 'apophaticism' of the poetic word or of figurative expression, within a culture of positivistic totalitarianism (by distinguishing between 'that which is said' and 'that which is only shown, the mystical element', according to Wittgenstein's formulation.[47]

---

45. Ibid., p. 17.
46. Ibid., pp. 17-19.
47. Ibid., p. 19. Yannaras cites here Wittgenstein's *Tractatus* 6. 522: '*Es gibt allerdings Unaussprechliches. Dies zeigt sich, es ist das Mystische*' (There are, indeed, things

In Yannaras' view the opposition between Eastern apophaticism and scientific positivism has not only been mitigated: 'It is noteworthy that, especially in the context of microphysics and genetic biology, one can speak of a kind of "apophaticism" of scientific knowledge.'[48] By way of example, he refers to the theory of relativity, in which the observation always depends on the position and movement of the observer; to Heisenberg's theory of interdeterminacy in which the observation always depends on the fact 'of the relation and the observer and the object observed';[49] to Niels Bohr's doctrine on the nature of electrons as both particle and wave; to the identity of mass and energy; to the notions of antimatter and the idea of the continuous generation of matter etc. Relying especially on Heisenberg, he writes:

> But indeterminacy and asymmetry are categories that refer *par excellence* to the space of personal unicity and dissimilarity, that is, to the personal dimension of the cosmos. The contemporary scientific conclusions of physics may constitute a point of departure for understanding the cosmos not as a mechanical order organised deterministically but as a universal harmony of infinite and indeterminate differentiations of a personal energy.[50]

Rationalistic gnoseology had already been questioned even in the philosophy of the twentieth century; Yannaras goes back to phenomenology and existentialism and refers to the studies of Nikos Nissiotis and his own research for *To ontologikon periechomenon*. He recognises that ontological inquiries into the philosophy of existence – their refusal to define essence ontically, the affirmation of the priority of existence with regard to the apprehension of objective essences – 'have contributed in a substantial manner to releasing Western thought from the impasse created by the long tradition of the objectivisation (*Verdinglichung*) of truth in intellectual definition or by the scholastic *adaequatio rei et intellectus*'.[51]

---

that cannot be put into words. They *make themselves manifest*. They are what is mystical [trans. Pears-McGuiness]). He cites it through an article dedicated to the *Tractatus* by Zisimos Lorentzatos.
48. Yannaras, *Hē apologētikē sta horia tēs orthodoxou theologias*, p. 20.
49. Ibid., p. 21.
50. Ibid., p. 22. Here Yannaras refers to the text which he was to produce in the same period, that is, *To prosōpo kai ho erōs*, a text which we shall examine in the next chapter.
51. Ibid., pp. 22-23.

The area of philosophy, however, in which gnoseological positivism seems to be discussed more profoundly and more radically is that which is constituted by logical positivism, analytical philosophy and the philosophy of language: 'Contrary to the vision of empiricist philosophy, where every theory must have its empirical authentication, the neopositivists seem to accept today that every empirical experience has its own theory and linguistic logic.'[52] Yannaras thus maintains that in this context a propitious time is available to us because Eastern apologetics has reclaimed a non rationalistic mode of speaking, its own iconological mode of speaking based on the irreducible difference between the word that utters and that which cannot be uttered by the word because it lies beyond it. The Fathers often use an antinomic manner of speaking (affirmation and negation of the same qualifier) to indicate that the knowledge of that which lies behind language is not possible by the use of linguistic categories:

> The common contemporary reference both to the intellectual affirmation and to the intellectual negation of the same signified object allowed a dynamic iconological imaging of the truth that is signified, that is, the overcoming of the exhaustion of knowledge in the coincidence of the concept with the thing conceived, the passage (*diabasē*) to another kind of knowledge, the instrument of which is not the conventional-ordinary linguistic idiom and its conceptual counterpart but an experiential-cognitive capacity in Man that is much more universal. This human cognitive capacity that is much more universal is the capacity for personal relation with what is signified, and it is to the realisation of this dynamic relation that the Icon calls us.[53]

---

52. Ibid., p. 25. In a note he cites R. Carnap and K. Popper.
53. Ibid., pp. 34-35.

Chapter III
From the Personalist Ontology of the Fathers to a Critical Ontology: between Theology and Philosophy

1. Person and Eros:
A Theological Essay in Post-Heideggerian Ontology

In the same year in which he prepared his essay on Heidegger and the Areopagitical writings – towards the end of 1966, according to his own testimony[1] – Yannaras began to be interested in the person from the ontological point of view.

This interest resulted in a doctorate in theology at the Faculty of Theology of the University of Thessaloniki.[2] He was awarded the

---

1. *To prosōpo kai ho erōs: Theologiko dokimio ontologias* (Person and eros: A theological essay on ontology) (Athens: Papazēsē, 1976), p. 10. There is an English translation by Norman Russell (based on the 1987 edition): *Person and Eros* (Brookline, MA: Holy Cross Orthodox Press, 2007).
2. Yannaras had previously submitted to the Faculty of Theology of the University of Athens a doctoral thesis prepared in Germany between 1964 and 1967 entitled *Hē metaphysikē tou sōmatos: Spoudē ston Iōannē tēs Klimakos* (The metaphysics of the body: A study on John Climacus), but without success. The thesis, Yannaras' first theological work, was published under the same title in Athens by the publisher Dōdōnē only in 1971. In the preface to this edition, dedicated to Dimitrios Koutroubis and Christos Kourouklis, Yannaras informs the reader of the events that had led to the rejection of the thesis (pp. 11-12). It was rejected in particular for the sharp polemics that he had conducted for some years against academic theology but also because of the high value given to the body and to eros within the context of a marked critique of any form of metaphysical and anthropological dualism: in Yannaras' view a certain dualism exists in Climacus but it is not

doctorate only in 1970 on the presentation of a thesis on 'The ontological content of the theological concept of the person'.³ The reactions provoked by this thesis⁴ led the author later to develop his thinking and – after partial publication in 1974 in the Greek philosophical journal *Deukalion* – give it mature expression in a revised edition of the work entitled *Person and Eros: A Theological Essay on Ontology*, a fundamental statement of Yannaras' personalism.⁵ Various lines of reflection that matured in the 1960s, such as those on corporality and eros,⁶ on the encounter between Western nihilism and Greek apophaticism and, finally, on his criticism of moralism both in the West and within Orthodoxy came together in this work.⁷

On this basis, Yannaras elaborated a notable reflection on the person, in which, on the one hand, he distances himself somewhat from Lossky and, on the other, seeks to respond to the questions raised by the thinking of Martin Heidegger.

His greatest novelty with respect to Lossky lies in his definition of the person. Indeed, despite underlining the apophatic character of the approach to the person,⁸ the whole work demonstrates rather a notable

---

an anthropological one or even a metaphysical one: 'it is a dualism between "in accordance with nature" and "contrary to nature", the nature that realises its goal through participating as a person in the life of God and the nature that dissipates itself in its rebellious self-sufficiency – in the end, a dualism between incorruptibility and corruption, between life and death' (pp. 10-11).

3. *To ontologikon periechomenon tēs theologikēs ennoias tou prosōpou*, published by the author in Athens in 1970. The title reveals how important the influence of Vladimir Lossky was.
4. Yannaras himself in *To prosōpo kai ho erōs*, p. 9, records the following reactions: R.D. Williams, 'The Theology of Personhood: A Study of the Thought of Christos Yannaras', in *Sobornost*, no. 6 (Winter 1972), pp. 415-30; the critical observations of Philip Sherrard in *Eastern Churches Review*, vol. 3, no. 3 (1971), pp. 356-57 and of A.M. Allchin in *Sobornost*, no. 1 (Summer 1970), pp. 53-54; and a personal letter from Hieromonk Athanasios Jevtic.
5. Yannaras considers the first edition of this work as *To ontologikon periechomenon tēs theologikēs ennoias tou prosōpou*; the second edition that of 1974 published by *Deukalion* in Athens; the third edition published in 1976 again in Athens by Papazēsēs. It is this edition that I cite. The fourth edition is that of Domos published again in Athens in 1987. This edition drops the subtitle, *A theological essay on ontology*. Domos again published the seventh edition in 2006.
6. Cf. Yannaras, *Hē metaphysikē tou sōmatos*.
7. Cf. Yannaras, *Hē eleutheria tou ēthous*.
8. Yannaras, *To prosōpo kai ho erōs*, § 7, pp. 38-40.

fidelity to the cataphatic method, supported by the etymology of the Greek term *prosōpon*.[9] In reality, driven by this cataphatic fidelity, he writes at the very beginning of his work:

> The person is defined as reference and relation and itself defines a reference and relation. . . . The sense which the term 'relation' acquires with regard to the person will be clarified gradually in what follows. At all events, it points not to an abstract analogy or comparison but to the fact of 'being-opposite-someone/something'. That which is 'opposite-someone/something', i.e. the person, certainly represents an individual, but an individual in relation, a dynamic actualisation of relationship. The relation is the 'specific differentia' of the person, the definition of the person, the radical differentiation of personhood from the sense of static individuality.[10]

At once, then, Yannaras goes far beyond Lossky's cautiousness with regard to the definability of the person and in particular with regard to the problems of defining the person as relation.

The person, then, is a relational event. Nevertheless, as in Lossky, it always remains an event which is not reducible to the totality of qualities that compose it, that which is common to all human beings, that is, to human nature. For Yannaras this perspective is thoroughly rooted in the Fathers: 'The ontological meaning which Greek patristic literature gave to the term is precisely absolute otherness as its existential difference from essence.'[11]

Absolute otherness with respect to *ousia* (which is precisely the totality of the totality of the features common to the individuals belonging to the species or rather the nature) nevertheless makes sense only as 'unique, dissimilar relation'; this absolute relational otherness, then, must be seen not as a describable object but as an 'event': the person is properly 'that mode of existence which is actualised as relation, not merely disclosed as relation.'[12]

In order better to clarify this vision of the person, which according to Yannaras has its origin in the thought of the Cappadocian Fathers and in Byzantine ontology,[13] he enters into dialogue with the philosophy

---

9. Ibid., § 1, p. 19 (Eng. trans., p. 5): 'The preposition *pros* ("towards") together with the noun ōpos (ōpos in the genitive), which means "eye", "face", "countenance", form the composite word *pros-ōpon*: I have my face turned towards someone or something; I am opposite someone or something. The word thus functioned initially as a term indicating an immediate reference, a relationship.'
10. Ibid.
11. Ibid., § 4, p. 32 (Eng. trans. pp. 16-17).
12. Ibid., § 5, p. 33 (Eng. trans., p. 18).
13. Ibid., Preface, p. 10. Yannaras declares that the aim of his work is precisely

of Heidegger and observes that in the final analysis the fundamental ontological question about beings and Being coincides with the question about the person, because the ontological question can be posited only within a relation between the person and beings, or rather the *alētheia* or the *lēthē* of beings lies in whether or not they are in relation with the person.

Consequently, even the Heideggerian *ek-stasē* is taken up in a particular manner:

> [it] is not confined to humanity's ability to 'stand outside' its natural identity, to wonder at its being, to conceive – alone amongst beings – of disclosure as temporality. *Ek-stasē* here is identified with the actualisation of the person's otherness, that is, with existential presupposition itself of the person which is also a unique ability to approach the mode of the existence of beings.[14]

Ek-stasē appears, in fact, as a key category for apprehending the otherness of the person and for understanding the significance of the energies in the patristic and Byzantine tradition:

to investigate 'the extensions of the ontology of the Byzantines, that is, the responses that they give in relation to contemporary research in the field of ontology'. In uttering these last words, Yannaras is thinking principally of Martin Heidegger. Note that in these years Yannaras uses the terms Byzantium and Byzantines without any particular problem. In subsequent years this changes. He prefers then to speak of the continuity of Greek ontological culture.

14. Yannaras, *To prosōpo kai ho erōs* § 6, p. 35 (Eng. trans., p. 20). On this point Nikolaos Loudovikos writes as follows: 'For Heidegger (who follows here the notion of the "I" as developed by Husserl in his phenomenology) it is transcendence that constitutes the self. It identifies Being with the *mode of existence* as *ek-stasē*, something which, as we shall see, greatly helped the Orthodox personalists to articulate their own views' (*Hoi tromoi tou prosōpou kai ta basana tou erōta: Kritikoi stochasmoi gia mia metaneōterikē theologikē ontologia* [The terrors of the person and the torments of eros: Critical thoughts towards a postmodern theological ontology] [Athens and Thessaloniki: Harmos, 2009], p. 19). Loudovikos has dedicated numerous pages to a critique of the Heideggerian point of departure in Yannaras' *Person and Eros* and the identification – in his view – of Heidegger's terminology with that of the Fathers. See Nikolaos Loudovikos, *Hē kleistē pneumatikotēta kai to noēma tou Heautou: Ho mystikismos tēs ischyos kai hē alētheia physeōs kai prosōpou* (A closed spirituality and the meaning of the self: The mysticism of power and the truth of nature and of the person) (Athens: Hellēnika Grammata, 1999), pp. 285-91. Yannaras has replied to this critique in *Hexi philosophikes zōgraphies*, pp. 124-34.

We know the essence (*ousia*) or nature (*physē*) only as the content of the person, and this unique power of knowing the nature signifies its ecstatic recapitulation in the fact of personal reference, the nature's power of 'standing-outside-itself', and becoming accessible and participable not as concept, but as personal uniqueness and dissimilarity. The nature's *ek-stasē*, however, cannot be identified with the nature, since the very experience of relation itself is an experience of non-identification. The *ek-stasē* is the mode by which the nature becomes accessible and known in the fact of personal otherness. It is the energy[15] of the nature, which is not identified either with its bearer or its result: 'The energy is neither the one operating, nor what is operated.'[16]

The role of energy and energies as manifestations of personal otherness beyond nature but not independently of nature (in some way they manifest nature as always 'im-personed') with reference both to divine reality and to human reality[17] – has been well understood and preserved in the East and in Palamism,[18] whereas in the West it has been lost as a result of the identification of God with a being (an ontic reality) and not with the person.[19]

15. The translation of the term *energeia* is particularly problematical. In *Protaseis kritikēs ontologias* (Propositions of a critical ontology) (Athens: Domos, 1985) 1. 111, p. 10, Yannaras defines the energies as 'the modes by which the subject perceives reality (both of the subject's own existence and that of objective things)'.
16. *To prosōpo kai ho erōs* §20, pp. 85-86 (Eng. trans., p. 57). The last citation is a text of Basil the Great that Yannaras takes from Gregory Palamas (J.-P. Migne, *Patrologia Graeca* 150, 1220D). Perhaps the clearest formulation that Yannaras offers in connection with person, nature and *ek-stasē* is the one we find in the preface to *To ontologikon periechomenon tēs theologikēs ennoias tou prosopou*, p. 7, where the person is called a 'manifestation of the ek-static possibility of *ousia*, the *universal* recapitulation of the *ousia* in ek-static personal existentiality'.
17. In the preface to *To ontologikon periechomenon tēs theologikēs ennoias tou prosopou*, p. 7, Yannaras highlights this existential correspondence between divine reality and human reality: 'the initial reality of the person recapitulates in patristic ontology both the truth of the mode of divine existentiality, the truth of trinitarian communion and the truth of human existentiality, the mode in which the order (*taxis*) of the divine life is reflected and imaged in humanity.'
18. Following in the footsteps of Vladimir Lossky, Yannaras retains – as we have also noted elsewhere – the distinction between divine Nature and divine Energy, 'the "specific difference" between Eastern Orthodox theology and every other theological or philosophical ontology' (*To prosōpo kai ho erōs* § 85, p. 327 [Eng. trans., p. 258]).
19. In the *Summa Theologica*, according to Yannaras, 'there is no reference... to the

It is from this ecstatic difference between person and nature that there emerges the sense of freedom, a sense in which there is a certain echo of Yannaras' meditation on Sartre:

> In earlier sections [writes Yannaras] I described nature as the content of the person, and person as nature's mode of existence, or the existential recapitulation of our nature as a whole (*katholikē*). The ecstatic otherness of the person is not defined by its nature, since it transcends (as otherness) the fixed boundaries of the common attributes that constitute the nature. But the person fixes the boundaries of its nature or *ousia*, since it constitutes nature's mode of existence. This means not that every human person is part of humanity's being, a part of human nature, but that it 'contains' the universal nature, or is the existential instantiation of that nature. Human nature exists only 'in persons', only in a personal *mode* (*tropos*), only as disclosure of personal otherness. Personal otherness is instantiated and disclosed with respect to the common attributes of nature. It presupposes the common nature, although it transcends it as an ecstatic fact in the case of every specific human existence.... The existential relation between person and nature presupposes their ontological difference. The person recapitulates the nature, as existential reality, without exhausting it and simultaneously transcends the nature, as ecstatic otherness – it determines the nature without being determined by it. The ontological difference between person and nature, the simultaneous existential identity and otherness, constitutes the single human existence as a specific existential fact of freedom: freedom of the person with regard to the nature, freedom of the determination of the nature by personal otherness....
>
> As the ontological difference between person and nature, freedom is an immediate experiential reality which is so specific as an existential potentiality that it can destroy itself. What we call

---

personal God of existential relation: there God is the object of rational inquiry, an abstract intellectual certainty, an ontic essence absolutely in actuality (*energitikē*), an impersonal and existentially inaccessible motive cause. By contrast, in the Greek East the question of the energies is posed exclusively within the context of existential experience. The Church's experience is the knowledge of God as a fact of personal relation, and the question that is posed concerns the witness to this fact and the defence of it, the question "how we know God not as an object of the mind, or of the senses, or anything else at all that belongs among beings'" (Dionysius the Areopagite, *De divinis nominibus* III, *Patrologia Graeca* 3, 869C; *To prosōpo kai ho erōs* § 20, p. 85 [Eng. trans., pp. 56-57]).

freedom is not simply our power to make rational choices among the possibilities presented to us, but the immense potential we have for the self-realisation of the person, a potential that destroys itself. The self-destruction of freedom, which is the most tragic way it has of affirming itself, signifies the voluntary subjection of the person to the impersonality of the nature. It is what we call the Fall, a deterioration or reversal of the primordial relation between person and nature, an existential alienation of their ontological difference.[20]

The ecstatic freedom of the human person is for Yannaras the very place of the possibility of *eros*. When in later years he felt compelled to respond to certain criticisms, he stated very clearly: 'In *Person and Eros* the fact of *ek-stasē*, following the Areopagitical writings, is identified with the existential possibility of *eros* (and indeed with *erōs ek-statikos*).' What he does is to set *ek-stasē* in relation to the *erōs* of the Greek Fathers which is the loving power and the movement of exodus from the atomically individualised mode of existence – in space, between objects – towards the actualisation of relationship *par excellence*: 'Eros is the dynamics of *ek-stasē*, which finds its consummation as personal reference to supreme Otherness: "divine eros is also *ek-statikos*, so that lovers belong not to themselves but to the beloved"'.[21]

Within this cognitive horizon, delineated by the ontological difference between persons and nature, beings cannot behave differently than in relation with the person because the person is 'the only possible relation with beings'; beings 'are manifested' and, consequently, 'are-present' only in relation to the person. Or rather, the human person is 'the presupposition of universal relation, in the context of which beings become true (*a-lētheuoun*), that is, they are disclosed as that which they are'.[22]

It is apparent that Yannaras seems to see in the idea of person-otherness-relation something that can be a better basis for certain Heideggerian categories, in particular the appearance of beings on the horizon of Being. From this point of view it is no wonder that, on the one hand, he reproaches Heidegger for remaining in a state of thought defined by 'the absence of understanding or experience of the fact of relation, that is, of the ontological priority of the person' and, on the other, presents his reflections as a reprise of Heidegger's thinking in light of the acquisition of the awareness of the person:

---

20. Ibid., § 77, pp. 297-98 (Eng. trans., pp. 232-33).
21. Ibid., § 6, p. 36 (Eng. trans., p. 20). The citation is from *De divinis nominibus* 4, XIII, *Patrologia Graeca* 3, 712.
22. *To prosōpo kai ho erōs*, § 8, p. 42 (Eng. trans., p. 25).

> With the ontological presuppositions of the Christian East we should understand disclosure as personal relation and nothingness as the absence of relation, whereupon it is no longer temporality but relation which defines the unique possibility of understanding Being as being-present (*par-ousia*). (We shall see in a later chapter how even temporality is a connection of personal relationship, the measure of relation). . . . We shall see in what follows that the person itself exists only as presence, but in the case of the referential presence of the person, the reference is actualised (ontologically – 'constitutively', not simply 'functionally') with regard to another not only personal but also *kata ousian* otherness.[23]

Beings, precisely in so far as they emerge as presence (*par-ousia*) on the cognitive horizon of the person, are not identified with Being but speak of Being to the person through being present to the person:

> Beings do not contain Being. Being is not their very self, the structured coherence of their properties. Beings witness to Being when they rise up in the space of personal relation. They refer to being as the content of the person. Consequently, we cannot separate the existence of beings from the mode by which they are what they are, i.e. from personal reference. The person is in relation to beings with regard to the principle (*logos*) of the *ousia* as *par-ousia* (presence). Person and beings compose the ontological, revelatory relation of Being.[24]

These words demonstrate Yannaras' desire not only to go beyond Heidegger but also to rediscover, by going over Heidegger's thought in a new mode, a path towards the transcendence of the divine. This desire appears suddenly in the following paragraphs in which he attempts a

---

23. Ibid., § 11, pp. 54-55 (Eng. trans., pp. 34-35). The chapter dedicated to time (chapter 3 of Part Two) bears the title: '*Hē prosōpikē diastasē tou chronou: Hē parousia*' (The personal dimension of time: Presence). Among other things Yannaras writes there: 'Ecstasy is "temporalised" as change; time is the understanding of ecstasy as change, the now conscious cognition of succession from *lēthē* to *a-lētheia*. This means that the consciousness of time is an experiential coordination of the disclosure of beings, the rising up of beings into personal relation' (ibid. § 46, p. 174 [Eng. trans., p. 130]). The chapter dedicated to space is chapter 2 of Part Two, with the title '*Hē prosōpikē diastasē tou chorou: Hē apousia*' (The personal dimension of space: Absence).
24. Ibid. § 11, p. 55 (Eng. trans., p. 35).

demonstration of a personal God, the God/*Logos*, precisely on the basis of the witness of beings. Indeed, the things that appear on the horizon of the human person 'testify to God the creator' like a house testifies to its builder: they are properly *pragmata-praxeis* and testify to being caused by a *praxē*: 'the principle (*logos*) of the presence (*par-ousia*) of "things", (*pragmatōn*), a principle of personal *praxē* which constitutes their cause (*aitia*), witnesses to the *prosōpo* of God without exhausting the determination of the divine *Prosōpo*.'[25] The *logos* of things/*pragmata* and the call (*klēsē*) that summons every human being in a personal, unique and unrepeatable mode, 'to a relation that transcends the limitations of space and time'; a call that makes the existence of a personal God/*Logos* known.[26]

True knowledge of such a God/*Logos*, however, cannot simply be a piece of purely rational reasoning, or simply be the result of inductive reflection on the first cause of beings. It is accomplished in the actualisation of the awareness of a summons, that is, in 'the actualisation of an exclusive relation, of an immediate communion which is an event of ecstatic reciprocity, that is, of reciprocal loving-erotic self-offering'.

For this personal character of the encounter between Man and the awareness of things/beings/*pragmata*, it is necessary that the knowledge of the truth of the God/*Logos* should be identified 'with the experience of personal universality – an experience of ecstatic-erotic self-transcendence'.

Nevertheless, the first move belongs to God, to his own ecstatic existence, to his loving will to offer himself as relation of personal communion; it is for this reason, Yannaras observes, that it is precisely in 'loving-self-offering' that humanity is revealed as an image of God.[27]

Humanity – in this light – exists as a response to a summons and is therefore never reducible to a mere being-there (in Heidegger's words a response to *Da-sein*).[28] Indeed, Yannaras writes:

---

25. Ibid. § 13, p. 60 (Eng. trans., p. 40). At note 70 of the same page Yannaras says: 'One may observe that by referring every form of matter ultimately to a form of energy (contemporary physics attests to the character of beings as "*pragmata*") reveals the creation of the universe as a *praxē* that is accomplished.' Observe that the Greek term to indicate 'things' is precisely *pragmata*, which indicates linguistically that which is given as a result of a *prattein*, or an act that is performed.
26. Ibid.
27. Ibid. § 13, pp. 60-61 (Eng. trans., p. 41).
28. Ibid. § 83, p. 317 (Eng. trans., p. 250): 'the mode by which we know the reality of the human person is not by studying humanity's specific being-there ("*Da-sein*"), because this can be exhausted within the limits of individual distantiality (*apo-stasē*).'

And since the person is the response to the summons to an ecstatic relation, it is the summons that defines its existential grounds. Consequently, the truth of the person lies beyond the given being-there in the world of individual existence. It lies in the fact of the summons which defines the person as an *ek-static* potentiality.[29]

Such a summons – 'a fundamental potentiality of the person . . . beyond the limits of the distantiality (*apo-stasē*) of ontic individualities' – is precisely a 'personal presence which transcends the being-there in the world of individual existence. This is why [Yannaras adds] in the theology of the Christian East we approach the reality of the human person from the starting-point of the revealed truth of a personal God.' Thus, the reference to God is the basis of the origin and the end of Man in so far as he or she is person.[30]

This transition from philosophical reflections to theological conclusions is puzzling; it is not apparent how such a transition is based logically on the idea of created beings as the result of a personal action, on the idea of their being a summons to communion with God. Here, however, it is useful to recall both the subtitle of the book (a theological essay, at least by the time of the 1976 edition) and Yannaras' firm conviction that in the Greek tradition there is not a rigid separation between theology and philosophy.[31]

This method of the theological use of philosophical categories gives particularly brilliant results – in my opinion – in the treatment of the problems of the Fall or of humanity's inauthentic condition, which in reality is very far from its personal truth. Indeed, in speaking of this Yannaras brings the truth of belief in original sin into relation with the way in which Heidegger and Sartre discuss the Fall, interweaving it with patristic perspectives (Dionysius the Areopagite, Isaac the Syrian and Maximus the Confessor) and opening up a rigorous ontologico-personalistic understanding of the whole economy of salvation.

---

29. Ibid. § 83, p. 317 (Eng. trans., p. 250).
30. Ibid. Here Yannaras cites Vladimir Lossky.
31. *Schediasma eisagōgēs stē philosophia*, vol. 2, p. 60 (Eng. trans., p. 197): 'Naturally, Western European historiography and philosophy, with the strict separation and contrast they introduced between theology and philosophy (a contrast unknown and unintelligible to the Greek world in both pre-Christian and Christian times), were ignorant for many centuries of the philosophical contribution of Greek theologians of the early and middle Christian period – just as they were also ignorant to a large extent of the theological character of ancient Greek philosophical literature, usually restricting the contribution of the Greeks to the sector of epistemological method alone.'

In Heidegger, as in Sartre, the Fall in reality has a significance which is ontological and not purely moral:

> The Fall (*Verfall, Verfallen, Verfallenheit*) is an uninterrupted falling away of human existence from its authentic self-motivated existential potentiality to a neutralised 'world' of 'everydayness' – a falling away from being (*Sein*) to being-with-another (*Miteinandersein*) in the space of coexistence. This coexistence constantly neutralises humanity's being, creating a 'middle term' of our presence-in-the-world (*Durchschnittlichkeit des Daseins*, or 'averageness of *Dasein*'). In the context of 'everydayness' the mode is disclosed by which individual existence (*Alltäglichkeit des Daseins*, or 'everydayness of *Dasein*') also usually is by a middle term, and this mode is the neutralised unit of coexistence, the neutral Man, or 'somebody'. The 'somebody' is not anybody specifically, and although it is all of us, it is all of us not as a whole, but as disclosures of the mode by which anybody-is in everydayness.[32]

For Sartre, on the other hand, from whom Yannaras sites a celebrated passage from *L'Être et le Néant*, it is the feeling of shame that reveals the event of the Fall:

> Shame is a sense of the original Fall, not because I have committed this or that transgression, but simply because I have fallen into a world, among things, and need the mediation of the 'other' in order to be that which I am.... To dress yourself means to cover your objectivity, to claim the right to see without being seen, that is, to be only a subject. That is why the biblical symbol of the Fall, after the original sin was committed, is the fact that Adam and Eve knew that they were naked.[33]

Thus Yannaras sees in these two descriptions a basis for giving an ontological interpretation – not unlike that of Vladimir Lossky – of the Fall: it becomes the transition from person to individual, from a mode of existence that is ecstatic and in loving communion to a mode of existence that is atomised and fragmented; it is the freedom of the person negated in so far as the person is a person.

---

32. *To prosopo kai ho erōs* § 76, pp. 291-92 (Eng. trans., pp. 227-28).
33. Ibid. § 81, pp. 310 (Eng. trans., pp. 243-44).

The person [writes Yannaras] is subjected to the nature and is defined by the nature. It becomes an atomic individual (*atomos*) – an impersonal unit of the nature. The determination of the person by the nature signifies the deterioration of the ecstatic reference of existence, which ceases to transcend nature and is exhausted within the bounds of its natural identity. It signifies the existential alienation of personal otherness, the dominance of the common attributes of the nature over the uniqueness and dissimilarity of the person. Ecstatic transcendence of the nature in the fact of personal otherness degenerates into an *ek-stasē* of the individual within the bounds of the nature – and the antithetical *ek-staseis* of the individual entities within the bounds of the common nature divide up the nature, fragmenting it into small pieces.³⁴

Sartre's shame becomes in Yannaras 'the defence of atomic individuality against its objectification, the claim of its freedom to remain subjective within the limits of an objectified nature' and it is truly a sign of the Fall because 'in the personal mode of prelapsarian existence' there existed no defence against objectification since there was no need for it; in this condition the body was a 'complete expression and disclosure of personal otherness, a potentiality for universal loving relation and self-offering, a dynamic summons to the realisation of mutual ecstatic self-transcendence and communion'.³⁵

Yannaras, then, goes beyond Heidegger because in the German thinker, according to Yannaras, coexistence seems to be alienation, whereas one ought to say that the alienated mode of coexistence is the result of the distortion or the Fall of the ontological reality of the person; indeed, only the person 'counters the *apostasē* (the falling away) of atomic individualities and bridges the gulf between the part and the whole, between otherness and universality, between a specific dissimilar, unique and unrepeatable existence and human nature in general'.³⁶

---

34. Ibid. § 77, p. 298 (Eng. trans., p. 234).
35. Ibid. § 81, pp. 310-11 (Eng. trans., p. 244).
36. Ibid. § 76, p. 294 (Eng. trans., p. 230). The postlapsarian condition, in which the other is distant, 'the confirmation of my existential failure', is hell in the sense in which Sartre asserts that 'hell is other people' (Ibid., p. 336; Eng. trans., p. 266). Yannaras comments: 'The "other" is hell because he torments me by revealing the condemnation that is my "freedom", that is to say, the tragic loneliness of my existential self-containedness, my inability to relate to the "other", and consequently the irrationality of my existence, the impossibility of dialogue, my incapacity to express love. That which is outside of personal ecstasy is shown to be an abyss of atomic distantiality,

It is not difficult for Yannaras to find passages in the Fathers to demonstrate that they had already intuited this personalistic-ontological meaning of the Fall; I note here just a single text, one of Maximus the Confessor, which reads: 'The one nature has been divided into a myriad fragments and we who belong to this one nature are victims of one another like vicious serpents.'[37]

The economy of salvation can therefore be understood – in this context – only as the restoration of a personal mode of existence and it is in this way that Yannaras actually views the matter, setting at the centre of the salvation of the human person – now subjected to nature – the person of Christ. Indeed, in Christ:

> the ecstatic reference of human nature to its existential *telos* was restored (the *telos* being a living communion with the uncreated cause and fullness of life, with the unlimited duration of life) so that what was restored was humanity's immediate universal (catholic) relation to God and communion with him. This communion is the principle (*logos*) of existence, its meaning, its cause and, at the same time, the goal and fullness of its truth. Every ontological and existential theory is made whole in Christ because he is the *Logos* of every existing and existential reality. He is the *Logos*-hypostatic revelation of God, but also the *logos* of created beings, the disclosure of God's personal creative energy. He is also the *logos* of human existence, its existential *telos* and meaning – the recapitulation of the 'logical' harmony of the world and of the *logos* of history in God's relation with humanity.[38]

Christ, then, has an essential primacy and centrality with regard to the creature: he is the meaning of everything and of history because in him, the man-God and *Logos* of God, divine-human communion, the ultimate purpose of existence, is accomplished. This accomplishment is not something that is attained but is a 'nature' that is the goal from the beginning, that is to say, is a given in the human-divine nature of Christ. Thus, Man can be saved from the hell of impersonal existence, a monad amongst monads, only by approaching the gift of God in Christ:

---

a hell of tragic and insurmountable loneliness' (ibid.; Eng. trans., pp. 266-67).

37. *Patrologia Graeca* 90, 256B; Cf. *To prosopo kai ho erōs* § 86, p. 334.
38. Ibid. § 87, p. 338 (Eng. trans., p. 268).

> The possibility of the ecstatic mode of existence [writes Yannaras] the personal possibility of ecstatic otherness with regard to nature, which after the Fall had been condemned to be exhausted within the limits of nature itself as individual distantiality – this personal ecstasy of nature outside-of-nature now becomes a natural possibility within the bounds of the theanthropic nature of Christ.[39]

Man can therefore become a person in Christ by participating in the personal mode of existence of Christ's human nature, and such participation is truly possible in consequence of the Incarnation and the economy of salvation. In Christ the new nature, the personified nature, is given, and all have access to it:

> This existential event of the natural union of divinity and humanity is a 'new' nature, that is to say, a new mode of existence – since we know the nature only as an existential fact. It is the 'new' theanthropic nature which has as its 'head', or its fundamental personal recapitulation, Christ himself, and as its 'members' all those who participate in the mode of existence which he inaugurated, all those who participate personally in the universal (catholic) natural union of divinity and humanity. The 'head' and the 'members' form a body, the body of the Church, the concrete realisation of the 'new' nature of the incarnate *Logos*, the ontological reality of a new mode of existence – new compared to the mode of existence of a nature fragmented into atomic individuals. The Church is a 'gathering together of those previously scattered' atomic individuals of fragmented nature into the unity of personal loving *perichoresis* and existential communion with God.[40]

This Christo-ecclesial renewal of the personal mode of existence is a gift, a grace, with which God responds to Man's free will which, by renouncing its own self-sufficiency, moves towards communion with God.

From what we have said so far it has become evident that the Church is not a moral or sociological fact but an ontological reality and an existential event; it is the event-reality of the new human nature totally in communion with God and personified in Christ. This is what salvation essentially consists in, although it must be seen not simply as an instantaneous event but as a journey and a progressive conversion

---

39. Ibid. § 87, pp. 338-39 (Eng. trans., p. 268).
40. Ibid. § 87, p. 340 (Eng. trans., pp. 269-70).

of Man's old nature to the new humanity given in Christ and in the Church. The progressive character of this conversion allows us to understand the meaning of asceticism and of the sacraments in the Christian life. Yannaras dwells on this point in a text of exceptional density:

> By 'mystical life' I mean humanity's participation in the mysteries [in Western terms the sacraments] of the Church. And by a 'mystery', in the Church's parlance, I mean the mystical, that is, living, experience of that space in which human freedom encounters the Grace of God, which is dynamically actualised divine love. Responding to the love of God is not simply an emotional or moral event. It is the mode of personal existence, the mystery of humanity's existential communion with God. Thus the primordial mystery is the very body of the Church: human beings bring to the Church their free will, that is to say, their daily attempt, even if unsuccessful, to return to a mode of existence which is *kata physin*, to unity with other human beings and to communion with God. And they find in the Church the grace-filled complement of their own ineffective efforts, the total fulfilment of their goal. In the space of the mystery, human effort encounters divine love. Personal ascetic discipline or personal failure and sin are made good by the power of God, by the life which his love bestows. By the practice of such a dialectic, the image of the 'new man', the image of the citizen of the Kingdom, is gradually disclosed. The *ethos* of existential authenticity is revealed. Human beings bring to the Church every phase of their natural life, of their fallenness and failure. And each such approach finds in the Church a corresponding acceptance, a corresponding mystery of the encounter of human freedom with divine Grace. Each of the Church's mysteries offers the possibility of the human being's dynamic and repeated approach and incorporation into her life-giving body, into her theanthropic nature, into her authentic *ethos*. It is an event that transforms a life which is *para physin* into a life which is *kata physin*, which transforms the corruptible time of atomic existence into the incorruptible time of personal relation.[41]

There are only a few fundamental lines. These will be taken up and amply elaborated in a later work, the second edition of *Hē eleutheria*

---

41. Ibid. § 87, p. 341, n. 298 (Eng. trans., pp. 380-81, n. 39).

tou ēthous (The freedom of morality). In this work the thinking of *To prosōpo kai ho erōs* opens up a perspective of an intense ethics as an ontology of salvation in the personal mystery of Christ, the head of the Church.⁴²

2. A Hermeneutic Interval

The patristically-based post-Heideggerian ontology that lies at the heart of *To prosōpo kai ho erōs* comes to be progressively more precisely defined by Yannaras as a 'critical' ontology. In 1995 he was to say formally that the work *To prosōpo kai ho erōs* was the 'first theoretical stage' of his thinking, the starting-point, to be precise, of his early exposition 'of a critical ontology: that is to say, an attempt to reply to the question concerning existence (its meaning, its causal principle) that is subject to critical verification, to empirical falsification.'⁴³

The books that followed *To prosōpo kai ho erōs*, according to the author's explicit affirmation, aim to test 'the consequences of a critical ontology for the attribution of meaning to particular aspects of human life and the problems it poses (branches of the so-called "human sciences")'.⁴⁴

And these books do so in a quasi-systematic manner:

---

42. *Hē eleutheria tou* ēthous (Athens: Grēgorē, 1979, second edition). There is an English translation by Elizabeth Briere, *The Freedom of Morality* (Crestwood, NY: St Vladimir's Seminary Press, 1984). With respect to the first edition there are considerable differences. On the contents of this work, see Basilio Petrà, 'La teologia morale greco-ortodossa da Androutsos al rinnovamento contemporaneo', *Studia moralia* 22 (1984), and *Tra cielo e terra: Introduzione alla teologia morale ortodossa contemporanea* (Bologna: Dehoniane, 1992), pp. 95-100 and 187-92. Yannaras responds here to Zizioulas' views; on his relationship to Zizioulas, see also p. 25, note 30 above.
43. Christos Yannaras, *Prologos* in idem, *To rhēto kai to arrhēto. Ta glōssika oria realismou tēs metaphysikēs* (What can be said and what cannot be said. The linguistic limits of the realism of metaphysics) (Athens: Ikaros, 1999), p. 9. The echo of Popper's language is not by chance: Yannaras, *Kritikes Parembaseis*, pp. 107-08, asserts that he had also taken account of Popper in writing *Schediasma Eisagōgēs stē Philosophia*: 'I would venture to say that the writing of the *Schediasma* attempts to apply, within the context of a branch of theoretical science (such as the Introduction to Philosophy), the principle which was introduced by Popper for the empirical sciences and which we may call a principle or method of *diapseusimotēta* (potential falsifiability). The book aspires to be a "fundamental proposition" (a proposition that can be used as a hypothesis) for the explanation of the origin and the historical development of the philosophical fact, a proposition subject to refutation or non-verification.'
44. Yannaras, *To rhēto kai to arrhēto*, p. 10.

in the field of ethics (with *Hē eleutheria tou ēthous*), in gnoseology (with *Orthos logos kai koinonikē praktikē*), in historico-materialistic positivism (with *Protaseis kritikēs ontologias*), in economics (with *To pragmatiko kai to phantasiōdes stēn politikē oikonomia*), in postmodern cosmology (with *Meta-neōterike meta-physikē*) and in jurisprudence and politics (with *Hē apanthrōpia tou dikaiōmatos*).[45]

These are all works in which 'the propositions of a person-centred critical ontology' are put to the test. These propositions – as I have already emphasised – are taken: 'as a key for interpreting the "schism" which separated the Western European from the Greek philosophical tradition (*Schediasma eisagōgēs stē philosophia*).[46] They are tested as a basis for constructing a philosophy of the history of modern Hellenism (*Orthodoxia kai Dysē stē neōterē Hellada*).'[47]

In this putting of a critical ontology to the test, as is apparent, Yannaras also poses the problem of a metaphysics in postmodernity. Indeed, with *Meta-neōterikē meta-physikē* (Postmodern metaphysics) he sets himself the aim of:

> Simply and solely tracing the possibility of drawing from the language of physics and psychology, for the first time a non-nihilistic 'critical' ontology: an ontology which is subject to critical verification, to empirical falsification, and which for that reason opens up another perspective of postmodernity at the opposite pole from decadent chatter about the 'deconstruction' of every meaning.[48]

---

45. Ibid.
46. The title imposed by the publisher of the French translation of this work is *Philosophie sans rupture* (Geneva: Labor et Fides, 1984). The rupture is that constituted by the development of Western rationalism. The title of the English translation (which was chosen by Yannaras himself) is *The Schism in Philosophy: The Hellenic Perspective and its Western Reversal* (Brookline, MA: Holy Cross Orthodox Press, 2015).
47. Yannaras, *To rhēto kai to arrhēto*, p. 10. On *Orthodoxia kai Dysē stē neōterē Hellada*, which Yannaras not inappropriately calls 'a philosophy of the history of modern Hellenism', and which is a historical interpretation of the relationship between Greek Orthodoxy as it has actually been lived and Orthodox theology from the fall of Constantinople until today, see Basilio Petrà, 'Dal pensiero della differenza al pensiero dell'unità: Nota su un'opera di Christos Yannaras', *Vivens homo* 6 (1995), pp. 163-80.
48. Christos Yannaras, '*Eis mikron gennaioi*': *Hodēgies chrēseōs* ('*Generous in small ways*': *Instructions for use*) (Athens: Patakē, 2003), p. 195. The words of the title in inverted commas are a quotation from Cavafy's poem, *Thermopylae*.

This description by Yannaras himself of his personal theoretical journey – following on from *To prosōpo kai ho erōs* – highlights his wish to present a rigorous and coherent continuity in his line of reflection, with the risk, however, of concealing the change of perspective that takes place in his thinking.

This is a change that is tacitly expressed by the dropping of the subtitle (*A theological essay on ontology*) of *To prosōpo kai ho erōs* in the fourth edition, that of 1987. Until the third edition (1976) inclusively, Yannaras does not use the language of a 'critical ontology'. His ontological horizon is still that which he described in an exemplary manner in the *Prologo* of his doctoral dissertation:

> The present work takes the form of a philosophical essay. Yet it only consists in a systematic elaboration of the conclusions of patristic thought on the initial themes of Trinitarian doctrine and anthropology. It is an attempt to take stock of the first principles of the ontology that flows from patristic doctrine, the fundamental replies of Orthodox theology to the ontological question, to the question on beings and Being, their relations and their differences. In patristic teaching the ontological question is not put in the terms of argumentative-objective definitions, it is not exhausted as a response to the coincidence of the concept with the object of thought (*adaequatio rei et intellectus*), but refers to the scope of the existential event, to the space of experiential truth, and therefore also is recapitulated in principle in the real distinctions between nature and person, nature and energy. . . . The ontology that flows from the fundamental truth of Orthodox theology is set out here not in the philosophical terminology of the patristic era but in the terms of contemporary philosophy, phenomenology, existentialism and the Heideggerian philosophy of existence.[49]

This transposition of patristic ontology into modern ontology is well expressed by the subtitle already noted, *A theological essay on ontology*.

Later, however, something changes, particularly from the beginning of the 1980s when Yannaras no longer limits himself to a contemporary transposition of patristic ontology but makes a different move; he seeks to retrieve the content of patristic ontology through a vast and serious effort to demonstrate the philosophical possibility of an ontology that is

---

49. Yannaras, *To ontologikon periechomenon tēs theologikēs ennoias tou prosōpou*, pp. 7-9.

non-nihilistic, and therefore post-Heideggerian, and at the same time an ontology that is post-Kantian, capable of coexisting, that is to say, with a 'critical verification'.[50] In other words, what has been elaborated earlier in the preceding works in reliance upon the ontology of the Greek Fathers, comes to be elaborated philosophically – in dialogue with Western philosophical thought – and through received philosophical categories, formally setting the Fathers to one side.

This does not mean that Yannaras would accept the 'Western' ejection of theology from the history of philosophy, as the description Yannaras gives of his own intellectual journey, and indeed his claim of philosophical value of Byzantine philosophy, also show. It simply means that he moves on to the level of contemporary Western philosophical thought in order to demonstrate – in the context of such thought – the possibility of the rigorous thinkability of a critical ontology with the content not different from that of a (transposed) patristic ontology. This type of approach is closely connected with a rereading of Greek philosophy and the Greek notion of truth, that in any case finds its own historical continuity in Byzantine philosophy. The fundamental work in this exercise of retrieval is probably *Orthos logos kai koinōnikē praktikē*, to which we now turn.

3. The Philosophical Elaboration of a 'Critical Ontology': the Possibility of an 'Apophatic rationalism': the Social Fruitfulness of Apophaticism

In Yannaras' *oeuvre*, *Orthos logos kai koinōnikē praktikē* constitutes a rather special work in which he confronts the problem of reason and its cognitive power, that is to say, the question of rationalism, by entering into dialogue with various forms of contemporary philosophy.

His point of departure is the simultaneous acceptance of two senses of rationalism. The first is that which is a 'fundamental sociological characteristic of Western European civilisation (of the mode of Western European life)';[51] the second is that which makes reference to its philosophical meaning as it has developed in the Middle Ages and in western European modernity and has found its adequate expression in Kant:

---

50. Christos Yannaras, *Orthos logos kai koinōnikē praktikē* (Correct reason and social practice) (Athens: Domos, 1984), p. 98.
51. Ibid., p. 13. Yannaras draws on Max Weber through Jürgen Habermas and his *Theorie des kommunikativen Handelns*.

Ratio does not simply correspond to truth but is identified with the possibility of truth. This identification owes its philosophical origin to Kant but has developed as a common element of the understanding of the sense of *ratio* within the context of the linguistic semantics that Western societies have shaped.[52]

The simultaneous assumption of the philosophical and sociological meaning of rationalism allows Yannaras to make a more adequate critical analysis of the relationship between rationalism and the liberation of Man/society. The scientific and philosophical rationalism of the Enlightenment indeed proposed the liberation of Man from metaphysical dogmatism and from mystical arbitrariness, demythologisation, freedom from the determinations of nature and instinct; in reality, on the level of Western social and technological development, rationalism with its pursuit of objectivity[53] has produced bonds of submission and has alienated Man, reducing him to an abstract 'human unit'[54] of a rational/rationalising process.

Citing the young Marx, Yannaras sees in the alienation of Man from his work, from the product of his work, from his relationship with the other, as well as in the rendering of the relations of production autonomous, a number of typical signs of rationalistic abstraction in relation to reality. In confirmation of the links between 'abstractive alienation and rationalisation',[55] Yannaras cites a series of authors such as Max Weber, Karl Popper, Herbert Marcuse, Max Horkheimer, Theodor Adorno and Jürgen Habermas. From Habermas he emphasises especially the idea of *Rationalisierung von oben*, which flows from the rendering of science/technology autonomous (no longer means but goals), expresses itself socially in 'a positivistic collective conscience that plays the role of a surrogate for bourgeois ideologies' and becomes a scientific organisation for the institutional articulation of social life, endowed with the undiscussed authority of scientific rationalism:

---

52. Yannaras, *Orthos logos kai koinōnikē praktikē*, p. 18.
53. Ibid., p. 32: 'Science in the context of Western society has claimed its independence of any bond of *a priori* authority, any dogmatic prejudgements, any mystical and mythopoeic arbitrariness. This independence has been pursued with a determined use of thought and rational judgement, which has laid claim to "objectivity": the overcoming of any subjectivism and relativism, the arrival at an impersonal neutrality – that is, at abstraction from any individual and circumstantial element capable of impeding the generalised avowal of rational "correctitude".'
54. Ibid., p. 31.
55. Ibid., p. 18.

The conclusion of this [writes Yannaras] is the absolutely abstract concept of the individual: individual existence becomes a function of a rationality that has been 'systematised' and made 'instrumental' and 'strategic' (*System-instrumentelle-strategische Rationalität*), realising its own life through some 'group identity'.[56]

By following these lines critical of capitalistic society and advanced industry, Yannaras dwells on technology as a logic of domination; what he is interested in bringing out is that, in its concrete application to economic and social processes, rationalism has become evermore a rationalism verified by its productive capacity – in every context – but measured by its productivity on the basis of rational criteria of verification with the result that rationalism allows no alternative.[57] The result of this line of development is political totalitarianism or totalitarian organisation.[58]

The social line of development of Western rationalism has been accompanied by the philosophical development of rational dogmatism which has its roots in Kant[59] and has subsequently assumed various forms different from its origins, such as '*absolute positivism, determinism, and pure scientism or the fetishism of science*'.[60] Yannaras dedicates many pages to criticising these forms, citing authors already mentioned as well as Sigmund Freud and Cornelius Castoriadis, and underlining that in so doing he has absolutely no wish to 'eliminate from everyday practice and cultural and political dynamic the use of correct reason and science'.[61]

His critique turns in the first instance to what he calls a 'consistent criticism' (based 'on the critical capacity and function of the human subject'),[62] not so much on the Kantian critique which he has already

---

56. Ibid., p. 40.
57. Ibid., p. 45: 'This rational organisation of the production of a work is the fundamental product of scientific technology and functions socially as an obvious presupposition of the ameliorative "development" and positive "progress" of human life. It constitutes the first and undiscussed need in societies of the Western type, a *need* to which all the other exigencies are subjected.' Yannaras refers the reader to *Dialectic of Enlightenment* of Theodor Adorno and Max Horkheimer.
58. *Orthos logos kai koinōnikē praktikē*, p. 45.
59. Ibid., p. 48: in Kant 'dogmatic authority is transferred from truth in itself to truth with-regard-to-us, to the objectivity of truth which is assured by an abstractive reduction to the outcome of the subjective intellectual exigencies'.
60. Ibid., p. 50. The italics are the author's.
61. Ibid., p. 76.
62. Ibid., p. 77.

touched on, as on the critique which he calls 'the second current of criticism which began with Marx: with his critique of the political economy Marx inaugurated a gnoseological criticism that turned on its head the objective intellectual forms for determining truth, moving the verification of knowledge to the critical clarification of the ongoing social dialectic.'[63]

Basing himself on the Frankfurt School, Yannaras demonstrates the dogmatic and authoritarian implications of Marxism; he maintains, however, that even such a school remains ensnared in the dogmatic consequences 'of the negation of every ontological foundation of the critique'.[64] Even the attempt of Jürgen Habermas to safeguard a critical approach to reality and to truth by retrieving Kant's moral imperative is not free from the threat of dogmatism. He then pays great attention to the works of Karl Popper and his attempt – unsuccessful in Yannaras' view – to avoid scepticism.[65]

Yannaras does not subject this criticism to a critique in so far as it makes use of correct reasoning as the Greeks call it; he subjects it to a critique in its modern Western European form, for the ontological void that it reveals and for its bankruptcy. Indeed, this criticism, devised to assure Man's autonomy and therefore his liberation, in reality 'is not capable of assuming or safeguarding even its own great achievement, which is Man's individual and collective autonomy'.[66] What is needed is a retrieval of ontology, but it must be a critical ontology.

Indeed, for Yannaras, even if the criticism is bankrupt, nevertheless:

> it has opened up a path (even if it is only a blind alley) towards the autonomy of European Man, his liberation from dogmatism and despotism. In the measure in which we participate in the Western European mode of life (Western European culture with its global dimensions) we travel down this path and probably will continue to travel down it right to the end. Because the question today in philosophy is not the rejection of the criticism, or its 'myopic' improvements, but the possibility of an ontological foundation for it. Only this can save both the criticism and the

---

63. Ibid., pp. 77-78.
64. Ibid., p. 82.
65. Ibid., p. 90: 'It is difficult to doubt the fact that with Popper gnoseology and epistemology, in particular, have indeed arrived at a high point of a dynamic but also social (functional) understanding of knowledge. What can be more easily questioned, however, is Popper's optimism with regard to victory over scepticism (and by extension over pessimism and nihilism) within the context of a Western European type of society.'
66. Ibid., p. 97.

philosophy. And the question is this: can a critical ontology exist? Is it possible to give a reply to the ontological question, to the question of what beings and Being are, concerning their relationship and their difference, a reply that is offered as a basis for the universal consideration of the existent, by the explanation of the cosmos and of history, and which at the same time is not fixed in definitive concepts but safeguards the dynamic of a critical verification? Is a theoretical consideration possible that interprets the onticity of beings (the subject-object relation) positively without tying it to an irrevocable concept – a reply that liberates the perception of onticity, the interpretation of the existent, from every blinding predetermination and permits a cognitive access to beings and Being, ever subject to a fuller understanding? Is the ontological interpretation of the existent possible without reduction to a causal principle determinative of Being and becoming, a principle that does not constitute an *a priori* necessity of a deterministic predetermination of the existential event, but rather critically verifies the existential event as an achievement of freedom? Is it possible to reduce the existent to otherness with regard to any predetermination and to freedom from every necessity – is it possible to overcome the antithesis (and the conceptual contradiction) between freedom and causal principle, the dynamic of the realisation of the existential event and, consequently, the exclusion of any *a priori* concept of truth?[67]

The search for a critical ontology is conducted by Yannaras after looking first at Marxism and then at the psychoanalysis of Jacques Lacan. He looks at Marxism because Marxism is a critical approach and at the same time something more than simply a gnoseological critique: 'it is worth examining whether this "something more" constitutes or can constitute the basis for an ontological reflection.'[68] For Yannaras there is no doubt that this is the case:

In Marx's *Frühschriften* the notion of relation assumes a character that is clearly ontological while at the same time drawing the verification of its conceptual content from immediate *praxis* – the experience of subjective, social and historical practice. We say that the notion of relation assumes an ontological character

---

67. Ibid., pp. 97-98.
68. Ibid., p. 103.

because it defines the *hypostasis* (real and concrete existence) of the human subject in principle. . . . This notion refers not to the phenomenology of human behaviour, nor to some 'property' or 'capacity' of the human subject, but to that which Man is, to his mode of existence. The meaning of human existence as an event of relation is analysed by Marx on four levels: on the level of biological individuality, on the level of consciousness, on the level of personal energy or creativity and on the level of social coexistence.[69]

The centrality of the notion of relation as well as the possibility of verification on the level of practice is in some way, according to Yannaras, also present in Jacques Lacan (1901-81). In the (fragmentary) Marxist texts that are scrutinised, as well as in those of Lacan, there emerges a 'common element', that is to say, 'both the meaning of the manifestation of the subject as an event of relation and also the critical verification of such a meaning in the praxis of alienation'. With regard to Lacan, Yannaras expresses the wish to set out certain conclusions from fragments of his ('often enigmatic') thought on three levels: 'The level of the referential character of the unconscious, the level of desire as the original nucleus of the event of relation, and the level of a more specific definition of alienation as the submission of the subject to the signified, that is, to definitive cognitive schemes.'[70]

In this way Marx and Lacan become points of departure for the initial perspective of critical ontology, an ontology in a critical context. Yannaras recognises this explicitly, especially when he offers the reader a kind of summary of his line of argument:

> (a) We have accepted criticism such as the possibility of using correct reasoning, which always admits a control of verification or refutation, and rejects the possibility that knowledge (and all its social applications) should be subjected to the arbitrariness of dogmatism or of any other logic of dominion.
> (b) We have sought the possibility of avoiding letting our criticism slip into scepticism and agnosticism. We have argued that an escape of this kind is not ultimately attainable without

---

69. Ibid.
70. Ibid., p. 140. The Lacanian text that Yannaras considers at some length is Jacques Lacan, *Le Séminaire, Livre XI* (Paris: Seuil, 1973) (English translation: Jacques-Alain Miller, ed., *The Four Fundamental Concepts of Psychoanalysis. The Seminar of Jacques Lacan, Book XI* [New York: Norton, 1998]).

accepting criteria that flow from the ontological sense of truth.

(c) We have posed the question whether it is possible to formulate an ontological concept of truth that does not exclude the possibility of its critical control, whether the existential event can be defined and explained in a way that can admit a critical verification.

(d) We have determined the fundamental coordinates of a critical ontology of this kind (an ontological basis of criticism) through elements from the thinking of Marx and Lacan: we have taken as an initial presupposition the definition and interpretation of the subject as an event of relation and we have identified as a criterion of the verification of the existential and cognitive experience of the subject the critical control of its social character.

(e) We have borne witness to the integrity (authenticity) of relation as an existential and cognitive fact, subject to a critical control through its socio-historical establishment on the scientific (analytical) indication of the margins (and symptoms) of the alienation of relation in dependence, subjection, dominion. A verification of this kind is a critical one because it equally also presupposes the possibility of non-alienation, that is, freedom as the ontological determination of the subject.[71]

This conjunction – supported by passages from Marx (the young Marx) and Lacan – between relation and social verification constitutes for Yannaras a link with the apophaticism of ancient Greek thought:

(f) We have argued that apophaticism, with its dynamic characteristics throughout the history of philosophy, verifies knowledge through the practice of communion and relation and we have set out a brief analysis of the ancient Greek understanding of *koinōnein-alētheuein*.[72]

If this is true, according to Yannaras, it becomes possible to conceive of an 'apophatic rationalism'.

From this comes the considerable power that he attains in demonstrating the possible correlation that may be posited between such an apophaticism and the gnoseological researches that are based on a coherent criticism.[73]

---

71. Yannaras, *Orthos logos kai koinōnikē praktikē*, pp. 210-11.
72. Ibid., p. 211.
73. Ibid., p. 212.

Yannaras' ample reflection carefully examines the apophatic elements present in Wittgenstein (The *Tractatus*) and in Popper (*The Open Society*), observing that both of them lead at least to the conclusion of:

> a pure negation of the absolutisation of logical positivism, and therefore adopt some apophatic solutions even if different from each other. Nevertheless [he observes] in both of them there is another common element with consequences worth noting for the dynamic of the apophatic method: their common point of departure is the exclusion of the possibility of the social production of knowledge.[74]

He then goes on to consider what he calls the impasse of the more coherent concepts of logical positivism and the effect that they can have on the 'meaning of apophatic gnoseology for contemporary epistemology'.[75] He passes under review Rudolf Carnap, William van Orman Quine, Andrew Tarski, Thomas S. Kuhn, Hilary Putnam and Imre Lakatos; he gives particular attention to Paul Karl Feyerabend's methodological anarchism. These analyses lead him to assert that:

> the developments of the last few decades both in the broader field of gnoseology and also in the more specific one of epistemology give a clear sketch of the dynamic perspective of a renewed philosophical apophaticism – even if the criteria of its determination and reception often remain unclear and confused. Moreover, there is no lack of stubborn resistance from dogmatic rationalism. This resistance conserves and reinforces the finality of control and the methodical necessities of the rationalisation of production. . . . Given this stubborn resistance, the perspective of philosophical apophaticism assumes the dynamics of a liberating event, of liberation on a level that is both personal-existential and also social. We are

---

74. Ibid., p. 232. Yet in a different way, in both 'the exclusion of a social production of knowledge (more clear or more moderate) exists and shows the lack of an ontological proposition linking *ginōskein-alētheuein* with *koinōnein*. We say that such has noteworthy consequences for the dynamic of the apophatic method because it is clear that it leaves the critical verification of knowledge (gnoseological criticism) solely to the invocation of ethical criteria for the passage from the scientific proposition to the acceptance of an accord or contract. Thus, the social functionality of knowledge always remains a good that is sought but with a clear character that is only practical' (ibid.).
75. Ibid., p. 233.

speaking of a dynamic of liberation. Precisely because the liberating character of apophaticism is neither obvious nor automatic.[76]

This philosophical apophaticism, which is rational but dogmatic can suggest several lines of liberation (from a rationalism that is dogmatic or subordinated to various forms of power), such as 'emancipation from the "ownership" of reason',[77] 'disengagement from a professional authority',[78] 'the balance between experience and reason'.[79]

Yannaras also attempts a description of the term 'apophatic rationalism':[80]

> Rationalism is apophatic when it does not exhaust the correctness of reasoning in the subjective success of coordinating thought with the structure and syntax of reality, and does not locate

---

76. Ibid., pp. 256-57.
77. Ibid., p. 258. 'Thus, knowledge and the methodology of knowledge acquire a character that is relative, but not in the sense of knowledge that is defective or doubtful in relation to an "absolute" and "indubitable" cognitive security. Here the term relative should be taken in a strict sense; it signifies the character of relation, the referential character that knowledge possesses – the reference to the mode of life and to the indefinite dynamic of this mode' (p. 262).
78. Ibid., p. 264. 'Apophatic disengagement from the professional authority of institutionalised scientific validity does not constitute another proposition – a methodologically or organisationally "better" one – or an ethical or *a priori* deontology that submits in its turn to scientific practice. Apophatic disengagement signifies a different *position* in relation to knowledge and a different concept of knowledge, the denial that knowledge becomes independent of the bearer of knowledge – the subject, which realises knowledge as a dynamic of relation. It thus signifies the denial that knowledge and the methodology of knowledge acquire a consistent autonomy like an economic good (*chrēma*) that is the object of a professional administration, like a private possession, a title, a privilege of power, a means of imposition' (Ibid., pp. 267-68).
79. Ibid., p. 268. 'The difference of a proposition that is purely apophatic is that the social functionality of correct reasoning is not accomplished when reason simply arrives at (or aspires to) an interpersonal accord, an agreement, or any kind of settlement, but when it constitutes or permits interpersonal relationship, even when it does not remove disagreements and antitheses. And the difference between agreement and relation is that in the latter we declare the possibility that the otherness and the freedom of every personal human existence is preserved and manifested – whereas agreement can be reached even by the passive acceptance of, or submission to, alien points of view. The point is not practical efficacy but existential authenticity, that is, the non-alienation of the human being' (Ibid., p. 275).
80. Ibid., p. 277.

rational correctness exclusively in object rules of syllogistic and demonstrative procedure. What we call apophatic is that use of reason that actually *apo-phaskei* (denies) all subjective or objective rationality *a priori* and draws its correctness from the dynamic widening of relation – both of the cognitive and productive/creative relationship of human beings with physical reality, and of the communal relations of coexistence between human beings. ... Rational apophaticism defines truth without ever exhausting it – truth is not exhausted in its rational formulation. Nevertheless, the rational formulation is required precisely because it preserves the possibility of a relationship with reason ... [81]

The consequences of such a philosophical perspective in the various fields of human existence, particularly in that of human social life (social practice), are innumerable and – says Yannaras – would require a systematic study of its own. Here he limits himself to considering the consequences that the apophatic concept of correct reasoning applied to freedom can have in political practice.

First, he dwells on the contradictory consequences that the cataphatic acceptance of freedom generates on the social level. Indeed, if freedom is defined as 'subjective possession and objective possibility', it can only be thought of as a 'possibility of making choices'.[82] This seems necessarily to lead to two forms of methodological practice.

The first tends to ensure the conditions through which one can manifest the initiative and independence of individual choices in various creative fields, particularly in the field of production and economic activity: 'A similar intention is inevitably implied in the claiming and realisation of choices: the freedom that every individual must have to "rise" socially, to occupy the position of the others – with the social phenomenon resulting from it that we call the class struggle.'[83]

The second methodological practice seeks to delimit the initiative and independence of individual choices – free competition – in such a way as to assure for all the fundamental and primary freedom, which is freedom from need:

A similar intention inevitably implies the interventionism of the central power in social life, an interventionism that necessarily leads to delimiting or dissolving many forms of individual

---

81. Ibid.
82. Ibid., p. 279.
83. Ibid., p. 280.

freedom, but nevertheless offers to all equally the possibility of the fundamental freedom from alienation, which privation brings with it, by abolishing the class struggle.[84]

Yannaras agrees with Karl Popper (and with F.A. von Hayek) that 'it is impossible to shape a project for society that is economically centralising and at the same time individualistic, that allows an effective state control of the economy (and in consequence also social injustice) and at the same time frees the initiative and independence of the individual'.[85]

The apophatic concept of freedom is very different because it is not reducible to the objective capacity to make subjective choices. It defines freedom as the 'negation of necessity', or it necessarily aims at 'the imposition on the subjects of elements of life that dominate it and prevent the subject from being fully itself'. Freedom '"negates" the alienation. It refers to the dynamic negation on the part of the subject of being something different from itself or, to put it in another way, freedom refers to the dynamic of the realisation of the identity of the individual.' Naturally, even identity must be understood apophatically: 'it signifies the otherness of the subject with regard to all that it itself is not. It signifies the unique, dissimilar and unrepeatable character of subjectivity – that which the subject does if it is that which it is – that is, freedom from every generic predetermination, from every dependent subordination, change and alteration.'[86]

The individual otherness of the subject must be thought of as unique but not in a monistic sense, but rather in a relational sense, because, as Yannaras has underlined in dialogue with Marx and Lacan, the subject is actualised in relation; both its realisation and its failure are relational. Therefore, in the case of the alienation of the subject, one must speak 'of a relation of dependence, of submission to necessity, of a relation of dominion, of a relation that is not free'.[87]

Therefore, one must not think that alienation is a danger that derives from outside the subject, or that it concerns a fixed condition. In reality, 'subjective otherness is alienated even on the level of natural homogenisation: of instinctive impersonal needs, of passions that are not controlled, of unconscious impulses' and freedom is a dynamic, a becoming, which signifies that even alienation can be overcome.[88]

---

84. Ibid.
85. Ibid., p. 281.
86. Ibid., pp. 282-83.
87. Ibid., p. 283.
88. Ibid., pp. 284-85.

According to Yannaras, a similarly apophatic concept of freedom, if applied, can lead to important results in the realm of political practice.

First of all, it can generate 'the demand for "direct democracy"'. Yannaras dedicates many pages to demonstrating the authentic revolutionary character of an apophatic concept of freedom, of a subjective exercise of freedom within the dynamic of personal relations in various communities. This cannot fail to lead to a much more universal participation in the responsibility for life in common. A responsibility that is focussed adequately, that is to say, apophatically:

> is not simply to do with a participation in the responsibility for choices but, above all, with a responsibility of relations through which subjective otherness is realised and manifested, while at the same time the authenticity, that is the social functionality of this realisation – the eventual alienation of the subjective otherness determined by necessity or finality that bind freedom – is judged. The measure of the critical control of the alienation is the distinction between [political] participation as a dynamic of relations (like the assumption of an individual responsibility in relation to the global realisation of social life) and participation as an intervention concerning a claim or programme designed to meet particular needs.[89]

Yannaras is aware that direct democracy is applicable only to a limited number of communities with sufficient economic means and that the principle of direct democracy is always seen as incurably utopian. Yet he observes:

> it will remain utopian until the moment when it does not become a fundamental and utterly imperative instance of assuming the character of a revolutionary objective, that is, until the moment when a large number of people become aware of the absolute priority of such a request and claim it without being worried about the necessary sacrifices.[90]

Moreover, it can lead to harmonising 'the productive process with subjective otherness', or with developing productive processes that are not alienating. In dialogue with Marx and Habermas, Yannaras deals

---

89. Ibid., pp. 285-86.
90. Ibid., p. 287.

at length with the question of the possibility of realising processes that do not alienate people but intensify their subjective otherness in relationship and in relations. He accepts as an irrefutable fact what the young Marx affirms, that is, that 'what alienates man is the lack of the element of personal creation in the practice of production. When work is not the expression of man's free creativity, the worker feels himself to be something extraneous to himself.'[91]

Yannaras also notes a third possible consequence of the application of the apophatic concept of freedom, that which he calls 'respect for failure'.[92] Indeed, in his view the appreciation of cataphatic logic to political practice does not offer a space for failure, because its aim is the pursuit of objective rational results: 'It must therefore exclude every individual failure or deviation from the common pursuit of predetermined goals. And the exclusion is realised either in the marginalisation of the deviant or in the violent repression of his deviation.'[93] In an apophatic logic, by contrast, there is:

> respect for failure and deviation or, more precisely, the very failure and deviation are shown to be organic elements of the dynamic of relations. Because failure as a rule is not the exception but rather the symptom that follows, in a greater or lesser degree, every individual initiative. The model of the 'perfect citizen' or the 'perfect human being' is found only in moral didactic handbooks and in the minds of the tyrants who seek to apply it.[94]

Yannaras dedicates these last considerations to the presupposition of that which he has asserted on the meaning of apophaticism for political practice, that is, the construction of political institutions capable of promoting an apophatic political process. He is well aware of the process of acquiring autonomy, to a greater or lesser degree, that is realised in social institutions (political, economic, educational, religious etc.) such as the growth of mechanisms of control, of bureaucracy, of the autonomous character of the economy and of politics in what he calls 'the cataphatic perspective'[95] of the organisation of society today. These are phenomena that also go well together because very emphatically they are reactions that occur on the socio-cultural level.

---

91. Ibid., p. 295.
92. Ibid., p. 313.
93. Ibid., p. 316.
94. Ibid., pp. 317-18.
95. Ibid., p. 324.

These reactions can open the way to an 'apophatic "art" of politics',[96] that neither totally negates that which the cataphatic perspective has produced nor totally accepts it:

> The point is still this, not that the way of confronting the autonomisation of institutions should not be decided and organised 'from outside', not that solutions should be imposed by the authority and the validity of a reasoning that is *a priori* 'correct', but that the solutions should flow organically from the logic of the relations, from dia-logical communality, from the dynamic of the overall harmonisation of needs and subjective aspirations.[97]

Still utopia? Yannaras is well aware of it, just as he is aware that it can appear a merely utopian perspective so long as it does not begin to be realised. Indeed, there is no predetermined objective guarantee:

> We repeat that a similar perspective still appears utopian today, precisely because the demand for the non-autonomisation and social functionality of institutions is not joined to the expression of a universal imperative need or because our faith in the possibility of cataphatic solutions has not yet been shaken in a decisive manner. The apophatic perspective presupposes a social leavening, perhaps a long one, but also a radical one and without compromises in its demands which will be nourished and activated through the ever fuller clarification of the goals that we can aspire to.[98]

4. Propositions of a Critical Ontology: *a 'Revisionist Empiricism'*

The possibility of a critical ontology, demonstrated on the basis both of a critique of modern thought and of the apophatic elements encountered in it, becomes the point of departure for an organic and, in some measure, systematic presentation of a formal ontological critique, which is embodied in *Protaseis kritikēs ontologias* (Propositions of a critical ontology).[99] The authors that Yannaras deals with are Karl Marx

---

96. Ibid., p. 332.
97. Ibid.
98. Ibid.
99. (Athens: Domos, 1985). The fourth edition (Athens: Ikaros, 2010) numbers the propositions differently.

(above all), taking into consideration not only the juvenile *Economic-Philosophical Manuscripts*, but also the *German Ideology* and *Das Kapital* (not discussed in the previous work), and also Karl Popper. With regard to Popper, however, his explicit presence here concerns the mind-brain problem rather than the works he co-authored with John Eccles. Nevertheless, the idea of verifiability (or falsifiability) remains central in this work, as Yannaras himself says.

The motive for this centrality is prompted by the primary object of the work, which is experience, and consequently the question of its foundation.

It is not by chance that these are the initial propositions of the volume:

> 1
> There exists a primary cognitive certainty – a certain (positive) knowledge commonly given and therefore universally valid: it is the self-awareness (*autepignōsē*) of subjectivity in every human being.
> 1.01
> Every human being has as a given the certainty that he or she exists, that he or she is a real existent. And that he or she exists as a subject, that is to say, as a presuppositional principle of every kind of knowledge: both of his or her own self-awareness and of the knowledge of any object whatsoever.
> 1.1
> Also commonly given is the experience (*empeiria*) of the modes (functions or energies) which assure and manifest subjective self-awareness and every other kind of knowledge. (Here we are using the term *empeiria* in the most primordial of the meanings which can be given to it: we identify *empeiria* with the very capacity of the subject to perceive, before any sense is attributed to the functions and products of perception.)
> 1.101
> The experience of the modes (functions or energies) which constitute and manifest the cognitive fact is the awareness of the fragmentation of the subject's capability of perception into partial 'capacities': the sensory perceptive capacity (by means of the senses), the intellectual (by means of the mind and its concepts), the critical (by means of judgements), the abstractive (by means of abstractions), the anagogic (by means of deductions), the sentimental and the intuitive capacities, the capacity for insight – and probably others.[100]

---

100. *Protaseis kritikēs ontologias*, pp. 9-10 (in the fourth edition these propositions

Yannaras' intention is to demonstrate that what is a given for human beings is their own subjectivity as freedom and otherness, a real experience that is always undergone within a relation and the dynamic of the relation. It is not by chance that he writes in his penultimate proposition:

> 8.21
> Philosophical ontology is a proposition for endowing human existence and its relations with sense – an attribution of sense to the mode of existence. And critical ontology bases its proposition on the existential self-awareness of the subject as experience of freedom and otherness. Freedom and otherness become accessible to us as cognitive-experiential fact through relation and the dynamic indeterminacy of relation. The criterion of the reality is the experience of relation with reality and the verification of the genuineness of the relation through its social broadening – the equally indeterminate dynamic of the social fact which constitutes history and culture.[101]

This conclusion shows that experience cannot be reduced solely to physical or biophysical causality, or to the pure mediation of the senses: it must have a range that is much broader and at the same time must maintain the verifiable character of real experience. In point of fact, Yannaras, in a very precise manner, sees the door that opens to a verification that is broader than experience in the primary connection between the experience of subjective self-awareness and relationality:

> 7.2
> When the support for the certification of the real is the initial possibility of its certification (the self-conscious existential experience of the subject), then the distinction between physics and metaphysics is removed, because the demand for objectivity is removed. The self-conscious existential experience of subjectivity is the point of departure universally (by all) verifiable, and consequently the primordial criterion of cognitive correctness for the interpretation of the existential fact – and we have seen in previous propositions that this experience is (from its very origins) an experience of referentiality: the knowledge of the existent is the existential experience of relation. Relation

---

are numbered 1, 1.1, 1.11 and 1.111).
101. Ibid., p. 156.

is verified by the mode which constitutes it as a cognitive fact, that is, by the broadening of the experience of referentiality, the intersubjective coordination of the experiences of relation: the communal fact.[102]

In order to indicate this philosophy of his experience, Yannaras used the term 'revisionist empiricism', which he finds preferable to any other. He also tells us why:

> 7.21
> ... Thus we can distinguish our proposition from monistic empiricism – which has as its criterion of cognitive correctness only the experience of the senses – and at the same time insists on its empirical character, excluding any false sliding into irrational mysticism (which is as arbitrary as materialistic monism).
> 7.22
> We speak of revisionist empiricism in our attempt to re-examine the hallowed practice of limiting experience only to the information of the individual senses. Even the initial (for the construction of the critical ontology) experience of the self-conscious 'I' (the existential experience of subjectivity) manifestly transcends the information of the senses. And this is not the only cognitive fact that emerges from experience, without being limited to the information of the senses. Using an entirely epigrammatic and inchoate formulation, we can say that every experience of relation is a cognitive fact which can arise from the information of the senses, but relation as cognitive experience is not exhausted in this information.[103]

This social (communal) way of verifying experience does not provide certain objectivity in the sense of indicating the *ob-jectum*, but this does not entirely signify that in this way a knowledge arises that is deprived of value.

> 7.23
> It should be becoming clear from the preceding propositions that disengagement from the Sisyphean demand for 'objectivity' does not necessarily also indicate a recourse to the subjectivism

---

102. Ibid. p. 34 (proposition 7.32 in the fourth edition).
103. Ibid., pp. 134–35 (propositions 7.33 and 7.331 in the fourth edition).

or relativism of knowledge. The opposite to objectivity is not the relativism of subjectivity (as it is also neither impulsive sentimentality or irrational mysticism). The opposite to objective knowledge is the communal verification of knowledge, the denial of the objective support of cognitive correctness – it is the intersubjective coordination of the experiences of relation, the communal validity of knowledge.[104]

The communal way of verification (not reducible certainly to the Marxist reading of Man within society), that is founded on the primariness of the connection between subjectivity and relation, thus constitutes the foundation of a critical ontology because it allows such an ontology a way of verifying its propositions. On the other hand, it is a way of verification that is not given but rather is realised. It is not surprising that the last proposition of the book is:

9

Truth for critical ontology is relation. And relation – consequently truth as well – is never a given. It is an attainment (*katorthōma*).[105]

It is evident that the notion of ontology is closely linked to the essential primariness of relation in rapport with subjectivity. That explains the important role that is also played here by Jacques Lacan with his *Le Séminaire, Livre XI*.

Propositions of a Critical Ontology is a philosophical work, intentionally and formally philosophical, as is *Correct Reason and Social Practice* which precedes it and to which Yannaras refers. In a manner not different from the latter work this nevertheless allows him to arrive at final conclusions that converge with those of *Person and Eros* – which in any case he cites[106] – and at the same time confirms the particularity of the Greek approach to the connection between *alētheuein* and *koinōnein*.

---

104. Ibid., pp. 138 (proposition 7.351 in the fourth edition).
105. Ibid., p. 179.
106. Ibid., pp. 122ff. Yannaras gives much attention to the role of Augustine in the history of Western rationalism and does not hesitate to refer to *To prosōpo kai ho erōs*, where he discusses the fetishistic concept of God and of the world. *Orthos logos kai koinōnikē praktikē* shows a greater concern to avoid any theological reference. One would search for it there in vain. Even where we would expect it – where he speaks of the *person* and of Greek thought – Yannaras avoids any direct reference (*Orthos logos kai koinōnikē praktikē*, p. 193, n. 1).

This allows Yannaras to assimilate *Person and Eros* to critical ontology (after the fourth edition the theological subtitle no longer appears), as we have seen, and at the same time allows him to deal with the various fields of knowledge through the medium of this type of philosophical ontology.[107]

---

107. Several times in recent years Yannaras has emphasised that *To prosōpo kai ho erōs* belongs to critical ontology. The latest example of this rereading, in *Hexi philosophikes zōgraphies*, pp. 220-21, is quite revealing. After citing *in toto* a passage from *To prosōpo kai ho erōs* on essence and energies, he adds: 'The above passage from *To prosōpo kai ho erōs* summarises the proposition of prosopocentric ontology as a "critical" ontology: a proposition interpreting the existential event that is subject to critical control, that is to say, that is open to the possibility of communal verification (or falsification) thanks to the realism of the distinctions between nature and person, nature and energies. After *To prosōpo kai ho erōs*, a series of studies seeks to test the proposition of a prosopocentric-critical ontology empirically (whether it is verified or falsified) on a variety of levels of shared experience: on that of the practice of jurisprudence, of political economy, of politics and institutions, of post-Newtonian epistemology, of normative ethics, of religion in contrast to the ecclesial event. In all these studies the presupposition of the realistic empiricism of the prosopocentric attribution of meaning in every area of human life is constantly repeated: the realisation and manifestation of personal otherness (that is, of freedom) thanks to the energies of nature, which are hypostatically expressed.' To each field there corresponds a particular work, which is explicitly cited.

CHAPTER IV

The Development of Reflection on Critical Ontology

1. *From* Person and Eros *to* What Can be Said and What Cannot be Said: *the Second 'Fundamental Stage' in Yannaras' Thought*

If *Person and Eros* constitutes the first formulation or stage of a *critical ontology* according to the words of Yannaras himself in his autobiographical account, a new phase was inaugurated in 1999 with the publication of *To rhēto kai to arrhēto*, as we have already mentioned.

'In the book which the reader now holds in his hands,' says Yannaras in the preface, 'I discern a second "stage" in the personal journey of my literary work.'[1]

What characterises this phase is the attempt to investigate the linguistic presuppositions of the affirmations themselves of critical ontology, or to research:

> criteria for distinguishing the real from the illusory character of the experience of relation (of knowledge which is shared and attained communally) in its given interweaving with language (and its objective functioning).
>
> Even the propositions of a critical ontology can signify illusory perceptions of relation that do not protect one from confusing the empirical realism of relation with the psychological surrogates of

---

1. Yannaras, *To rhēto kai to arrhēto*, p. 10.

real experience. The terms (and the propositions) may delimit the expression of feelings, not of significations that refer to the knowledge of what is signified. They may imprison the meaning of the signifiers in their common linguistic usage alone, in 'the mode in which this use is grafted (*eingreift*) onto our life' – the mode by which we learned to use the signifiers, but also to conjoin with them specific feelings of certainty, to live them (*erleben*) in a specific manner.²

The phrases with the words in German cited here are taken from the *Philosophische Grammatik* of Ludwig Wittgenstein (1889-1951) and refer to the fundamental thesis of the late Wittgenstein that traces the meaning of language back to its living usage, because language is a part of life.³ This is not an incidental remark. In this new phase of Yannaras, Wittgenstein takes on the role of a catalyst for his thinking.⁴

Yannaras does not dwell so much on the distinction between the early and late Wittgenstein, whom he reads rather as a unity and continuity. He is actually particularly interested in seeing how the experiential truth of ethical, aesthetic and religious language, or rather of the ethical, aesthetic and religious use of language, can be safeguarded without its meaning being exhausted simply by being lived (psychologically and sentimentally).

This is why Yannaras carefully recalls the 'neopositivistic' theses of Wittgenstein's celebrated *Tractatus Logico-Philosophicus* which seem to deny any real sense to such language:

> Thought, language and physical reality have a common rational articulation and structure [writes Yannaras in section 4.1 speaking specifically of the *Tractatus*].... The cognitive dynamic of Man's relation with reality has as its set limit this common rational articulation and structure. The limit of the possibilities of human knowledge is the world as the totality of facts (not of things)⁵ and language as the totality of propositions⁶ – where a

---

2. Ibid., pp. 10-11.
3. Ibid., pp. 25-28.
4. This is how Yannaras speaks of it in Ibid., pp. 11-12: 'In *prosōpo kai erōs* the spark or catalyst (the teacher's tracks) was for me the writings of Heidegger – what was most fruitful was the opposition to his propositions (not to his language or problematics). In the pages that follow the same role has been played by Wittgenstein.'
5. Wittgenstein, *Tractatus*, 1.1.
6. Ibid., 4. 001.

(linguistic) proposition is a (physical) picture of reality.[7] That which is outside of the world (that is, such as the sense of the world,[8] ethics and aesthetics,[9] absolute good and absolute value),[10] is also outside of language. Every effort to say the sense of the existent – moral and religious truths – adds nothing to our knowledge, is manifestly sense-less.[11]

Yannaras is nevertheless very clear that Wittgenstein is not on this level innocent of 'the logical positivism that considers any metaphysical research "devoid of philosophical sense"':

> his [Wittgenstein's] problem is the difference between saying and showing: 'there are, indeed, things that cannot be put into words. They make themselves manifest. They are what is mystical.'[12] Senselessness for Wittgenstein is this: to try to express that which cannot be expressed and is contained in one way or other in an unexpressed manner in what is expressed (to put in words truths that are aesthetic, moral and religious).[13]

That which Yannaras can evidently not accept is the linguistic prohibition (of the *Tractatus*) or the idea that the unexpressed must remain such and has to be incommunicable. In this last case it would become a psychological and subjective experience of which it would not be possible to say whether it was real or illusory.

Yannaras then looks at Basil the Great (330-379) and his critique of intellectual idolatry. Basil is clear that the experience of relation constituted by God's self-revelation cannot be substituted by intellectual notions that locate such experience in the customary forms of language: that would be idolatory. However, that does not mean that one is unable to say anything:

> For Basil the Great [Yannaras writes in section 4.3.1.2] (and for the Greek mentality) it is possible for the word God to refer to the second term of a personal (of the subject) relation and as

---

7. Ibid., 4. 01.
8. Ibid., 6. 41.
9. Ibid., 6. 421.
10. Wittgenstein, 'Lecture on Ethics', *Philosophical Review* 1 (1965), pp. 3-12.
11. Yannaras, *To rhēto kai to arrhēto*, p. 250.
12. Wittgenstein, *Tractatus*, 6. 522.
13. Yannaras, *To rhēto kai to arrhēto*, pp. 253-54.

a linguistic sign to function in correlation with the empirical cognitive immediacy of the relation. And then the verification of the referential function of the word is transferred to its communal confirmation: to the possibility that the truth of personal relation with the uncreated by every subject that has experience of this relation may be borne witness to.[14]

In this communicable connection with the experience of a relation, the word God can then assume the function of a symbol. Not in Wittgenstein's sense but in an etymological sense. It is in this difference with regard to the etymological sense that the fundamental limit of the *Tractatus* also lies.[15]

Indeed, for Yannaras the symbolic function of language precedes every other: 'Subjective experiences can be communicated by means of language when the linguistic signifiers function primarily as symbols and secondarily as intellectual meanings.'[16] The symbol etymologically is not, as Wittgenstein thinks, a sign endowed with sense,[17] but:

> the linguistic (or other) sign that *sym-ballei* (puts together, coordinates) single subjective experiences in a common reference to the same thing signified in a way that is experientially accessible. The symbol functions in every subject as a stimulus and point of departure for recalling and reliving the (unique and dissimilar) relations of every subject with what is specifically signified.[18]

The symbolic function of language opens up a greater degree of reality that the relational event possesses with respect to that which can be signified intellectually and said through the medium of language.

As it seems to Yannaras:

> Even Wittgenstein does not suspect that the greater (and more important) cognitive event is the experiential (*empeirikē*) immediacy of relation – the lesser (and derivative) cognitive event is the function of thought and language. He does not

---

14. Ibid., pp. 254-55. The author refers to a passage from a Basilian text of doubtful authenticity, *In Isaiam* 96, *Patrologia Graeca* 30, 276.
15. Yannaras, *To rhēto kai to arrhēto*, p. 38.
16. Ibid., p. 35, s. 4.1.
17. Ibid., p. 38, s. 5.2.1.
18. Ibid., p. 35, s. 4.1.

suspect that the knowledge which the experience of relation procures is signified – testified to and communicated by language but is never exhausted in the linguistic formulation (and for that reason is not identified with the linguistic formulation).[19]

It is in this broader area of experiential relation with respect to its linguistic formulation that a space is also found for metaphysical research. For 'if we forget the priority of relation, then language (the grammar of language) becomes the cage whose bars block any metaphysical research.'[20]

In forgetting this greater range of the experiences of the relation with regard to language, Wittengenstein shows – according to Yannaras – how he remains within boundaries that are typically Western, that is, the certainty 'that thought and language are the only possibility for a knowledge that is verifiable and communicable, because the *grammar* of language is the unique mirror of reality'. A certainty of this kind cannot but lead to the 'rejection of every possibility of metaphysics'.[21]

In the face of this typical Western certainty, Yannaras puts forward in section 4.4.1. the position that stays more faithful to the Greek and Christian tradition:

In the more brilliant cases of modern Western European philosophy (Kierkegaard, Heidegger, Wittgenstein) it becomes evident that the ontological void, or the ontological research of modern man has a clear gnoseological point of departure. Western man does not have at his disposal either historical-empirical habits, or even the acquired habits of the symbolic function of language, the approach to knowledge by means of the experience of relation (the participation [*methexis*] in the object of knowledge) or by means of the communal verification of cognitive relation (when all are of the same opinion and each testifies to it).[22]

Western man is not accustomed to the apophatic use of language, to refusing to exhaust cognitive experience in linguistic formulations, to having a positive cognitive experience – neither fantastic or illusory –

---

19. Ibid., p. 253, s. 4.3.
20. Ibid., p. 253, s. 4.3.1.
21. Ibid., p. 255, s. 4.4.
22. The author cites a fragment of Democritus preserved by Theophrastus, Diels-Kranz, *Die Fragmente der Vorsokratiker*, vol. 2, 119.

even with regard to everything that 'no eye has seen, nor ear heard, nor the human heart conceived' (1 Corinthians 2:9) with regard to the vision of 'things that are not to be told, that no mortal is permitted to repeat' (2 Corinthians 12:4).[23]

This participative, social or communal modality of knowledge as relation – not reducible to the linguistic formulation that constitutes the symbolic function of language – is that which is presupposed precisely by the ontological propositions and their rapport with reality.

In order to demonstrate this more effectively Yannaras chooses a field of analysis offered by a particular area of language: 'As a field of control for either the real or the illusory character of ontological propositions, what is proposed here is the language of references to the possibility of the existence of Man even after death.'[24]

In his view, the language of the Gospel regarding the life of man after death assumes real substance from the start of his consideration of the relational constitution of the human subject. In order fully to shed light on this constitution, Yannaras has recourse to an author who has accompanied him for decades, Jacques Lacan, and in particular to a phrase of his famous *Le Séminaire, Livre XI* – well known to Yannaras – which he renders thus: 'The subject is born in the measure in which the signifier is manifested in the field of the Other – the subject *in initio* begins in the place of the Other.'[25]

The subject is born through the work of relation; it is not reason that constitutes the relation but the contrary. In this is manifested that which is proper to Man:

> the possibility (that constitutes mode of existence) that the natural erotic impulse of life (*libido*) takes specific form in desire and in an instance of relation. We could signify this possibility (linguistically) as exo-physical (*exō-physikē*), because it is that which allows human beings to go in a direction opposite to the logic of natural adaptation,

as is shown by the striking case of anorexic children 'who self-direct themselves towards death', against every natural instinct of survival.[26]

---

23. Yannaras, *To rhēto kai to arrhēto*, p. 256, s. 4.4.1.
24. Yannaras, *To rhēto kai to arrhēto*, p. 11.
25. Lacan, *Le Séminaire, Livre XI*, pp. 180-81.
26. Yannaras, *To rhēto kai to arrhēto*, p. 122, ss 5.1.1 and 5.1.2. Yannaras takes his example from C. Castoriadis, *L'institution imaginaire de la société* (Paris: Seuil, 1975), p. 392: 'An anorexic infant lets itself die: its psyche is stronger than its

This mysterious given of a mode of existence that includes an exophysical possibility allows us 'the metaphysical hope', that is, the hope that:

> it is not only the rational subject that is the product of relation, but also that the ineffable 'core' of our existential hypostasis (which is known only in reference to the mode of relation) is the hypostatic response to an exo-physical call-to-relation (an existential factor of referential reciprocity, the term of a relation).[27]

It is precisely death and the reference to Lacan that return in *Ontologia tēs scheseōs* (Relational ontology), in which the resolution of being in relation comes to its fullest expression.

2. Relational Ontology[28]

If Heidegger was a catalyst for Yannaras' thought in *To prosōpo kai ho erōs* and Wittgenstein performed a similar role in *To rhēto kai to arrhēto*, we are probably not far wrong in saying that *Ontologia tēs scheseōs* is a book thought through, in large measure, within the horizon of some elements offered by Lacanian thought.

Yannaras finds in Lacan's psychoanalysis a line of thought – a clinically based line of thought – capable of assimilating the primary relevance of relation to the constitution of the human subject and also to the modality assumed by biological needs: everything in human beings is manifested as a form of the desire for life-as-relation, in the particular mode of *libido*. A phrase such as the following: 'By the term relation we define and delineate the generation and realisation of the rational subject in the space of the Other,'[29] shows the extent to which Yannaras found in Lacan many suggestions for the later articulation of his personalist ontology or his critical ontology.

The Lacanian horizon leads him inevitably to give consideration to sexuality and to deal with the naturalistic view of human sexuality. Yannaras gives it critical attention, starting precisely from the leap which *libido* manifests in the Lacanian perspective: from the impulse towards the desire for life-as-relation. The relational dynamic of desire arouses reason, constitutes a mode of being that goes beyond natural

---

biological control system.'
27. Yannaras, *To rhēto kai to arrhēto*, p. 123, s. 6.
28. Yannaras, *Ontologia tēs scheseōs* (Ontology of relation) (Athens: Ikaros, 2004). Eng. trans. *Relational Ontology* (Brookline, MA: Holy Cross Orthodox Press, 2011).
29. Ibid., p. 95, s. 9.3.1 (Eng. trans., p. 48).

determinisms (and is therefore in some way free), opening up to disinterest, to sacrifice, to love and to the discovery of otherness and beauty, or to the experiences of communion.

From the moment the subjective experience of relation necessarily includes consciousness, Yannaras dedicates numerous pages to dealing with certain data from the neurosciences and with the attempts to reduce consciousness to the brain, setting forth the evidence for the impossibility of such a reduction on the basis of neurobiology itself, of clinical psychology and of other data of human experience.

The analysis and affirmation of the primacy of relation in these contexts allows Yannaras to turn to some aspects of the Christian understanding of man, to some truths of faith. In particular, I would underline the analogy that he draws between the authenticity of the erotic relation and the authenticity of the relation of a human being with God (and of God with a human being): both are realised authentically when the encounter with the otherness of the Other occurs for its own sake.[30]

Indeed, the analogy between erotic relation and relation with God offers Yannaras the stimulus to ask himself what experiential occasions are able to be occasions of true relationship between man and God, also listing those which he considers criteria of an authentic relation:

> What could be the real – not illusory – occasions, the experiential starting points, for a possible relation between human beings and God? Could such occasions be those where relation fulfils the followings criteria: (1) implied reciprocity; (2) experiential access to the otherness of the Other; (3) transformation of an atomic mode of existence into an experience of sharing life in communion; and (if) freedom from dependence, subjection, utilitarian transaction, or convenient exploitation?[31]

A particular possibility is offered by the experience of beauty, of the attraction to relation that constitutes beauty as such. By this character of beauty to attract, perhaps more than the erotic experience itself, we are offered the certitude that may be a mode of existence independent of rational determinisms, a mode of existence as pure relation that can also allow us to speak of an ontology of relation or of relation as being.[32]

---

30. Cf. Ibid., p. 127, s. 12.5.4.
31. Ibid., p. 131, s. 13 (Eng. trans., p. 68).
32. Ibid., pp. 134-36 (Eng. trans., pp. 71-72).

The Development of Reflection on Critical Ontology

It is not by chance that Yannaras calls evil the non-beautiful and evil then becomes the subject of the author's reflection in the last chapters, in which evil always appears more as anti-relation, that is, the rupture/denial of relation and that which follows from it.[33]

This hermeneutic horizon of evil allows Yannaras to offer a new reading – and a very original one for an Orthodox writer – of the Fall in the articulation of which some Lacanian suggestions are used to good effect.

> The fall [writes Yannaras][34] is not attributed to the material or caused character of created beings. When I speak of the fall, I do not mean some temporal (i.e. occurring in historical time) transition from a higher to a lower level of existence; I do not mean a localised alienation but a comparative difference, a difference of distance from the fullness of life-as-relation. I compare our created existence, our experience of its ties and limitations, with the experience of the primordial desire that constitutes us as rational subjects – I compare createdness with the goal of the desire: life-as-relation, 'life which is immortal, life which is irrepressible, life which has no need for any organ, life which is simplified and indestructible'.[35]

The Fall thus becomes very like the birth of the rational subject in the space of the other, in that such a birth can only be in the distance from the Other:

> If the rational subject is born in the space of the Other, then rationality is a birth in the distance separating us from the Other. We experience this distance [says Yannaras once again][36] as a life-giving desire for its transcendence; we experience it as an existential defect, as a 'fall' that traps us in the law of death. But, thanks to this distance, or fall, the instinct for survival – an instinct that governs created being as a necessity – is constituted as a desire for life-as-relation, as an active (relatively free) management of self-transcending referentiality.

---

33. This reflection on evil is developed formally in Christos Yannaras, *To ainigma tou kakou* (The enigma of evil) (Athens: Ikaros, 2008). Eng. trans. *The Enigma of Evil* (Brookline, MA: Holy Cross Orthodox Press, 2012).
34. Yannaras, *Ontologia tēs scheseōs*, pp. 221-22, s. 20.2.1. (Eng. trans., p. 115).
35. The quotation is from Lacan: 'C'est la libido, en tant que pur instinct de vie, c'est-à-dire de vie immortelle, de vie irrépressible, de vie qui n'a besoin, elle, d'aucun organe, de vie simplifiée et indestructible' (Lacan, *Le Séminaire, Livre XI*, p. 180).
36. Yannaras, *Ontologia tēs scheseōs*, p. 221, s. 20.2 (Eng. trans., p. 115).

This challenge of Yannaras with regard to the Fall is associated with another one which is of equal significance. If the birth of the rational subject is not the fruit of a biological necessity, then we could ask ourselves why it should entail the death of the rational subject; why should the rationality mediated by cerebral functions ever have to come to an end because of the end of the cerebral mediation?

To respond to such a question – Yannaras notes – is for the time being beyond what is possible for us, even if the fundamental role of relation in the genesis of the rational subject has brought to the fore the determining functions of the Other. Certainly, one could ask: but is not this Other a projection of desire, a way of overcoming insecurity rather than a real second term of a relation? It is not easy to give a reply because a reply depends totally on the dynamic itself of the relation and of its personal experience. Yannaras notes that the Gospel message itself cannot give guarantees that are independent of the very dynamic of relation: even 'faith, or trust in God – who exercises providence, who is the giver of good things, the irradiator of sensible reality, the "bridegroom" and "most manic lover" of every human being – is always a personal adventure of verification without any *a priori* guarantee of certainty'.[37]

---

37. Ibid., p. 228, s. 20.3.5 (Eng. trans., p. 119).

CHAPTER V
Ontology and Salvation

1. Introductory Considerations

In the course of Yannaras' intellectual journey, as we have already seen, ontology became the axis of his thought from the time he left Greece to study in Germany and, given the rigorousness of his mode of procedure, it would be impossible to isolate any one of the positions he takes up from the ontological horizon.

Confronted with the challenge of Heidegger, the young Yannaras rediscovered the ontology implicit in the thinking of the Fathers and in the Eastern apophatic approach. Because of its origin, Yannaras' thought quickly takes shape as an ontology marked by the theological quality of reflection on the Fathers and is closely linked to salvation in God made man. It is not by chance that the fundamental work of his early years, *To prosōpo kai ho erōs*, is presented initially as 'a theological essay on ontology'.

The thinking of the years that follow – as we have emphasised – consists in elaborating an ontology that is philosophically self-sufficient, post-nihilistic and post-Heideggerian. On the one hand, this ontology supports a critical analysis of the various forms of contemporary dogmatic rationalism deriving from the Enlightenment, making ample use of the critical philosophies of the Frankfurt School and of Karl Popper; on the other, it enables the recovery and the rereading of the categories of Greek philosophy, on the assumption of the continuity – from ancient Greek thought to Christian thought – of certain Greek convictions: the coincidence between truth and communality and the non-exhaustion of the knowledge of reality in its formulation, that is to say, Eastern apophaticism.

The constant point of reference in Yannaras' intellectual journey, both before his conversion to ontology and after, has always been the West. From Dostoevsky's critique to the ontological critique the West has always been the term to be confronted, the negative side to be criticised but also to be saved. Or, perhaps better put, it is the thinkers marked by the Western mode of existence who transform God and Man into ontic objects, losing the sense of veridicality.

This point must be strongly emphasised because, if what is at issue for Yannaras, namely, the salvation of human existence, of each and every human being, is obscured, his critique of the West becomes simple anti-Westernism, whereas in the perspective of salvation it becomes a re-opening to a thinking that corresponds with humanity's *via salutis*.

Within this perspective something that stays with Yannaras is his youthful attachment to Dostoevsky. His conversion to ontology, however, marks the acquisition of an awareness that the salvation of the West entails its salvation from the ontological error that has been embodied in Western European history and has been expressed first in philosophico-theological/religious terms and then in philosophical/secularist terms. This is an ontological error in its consequences which first embraced the Christian East – even if not totally, for the East has tried to avoid it by means of the schism – and then the entire world, because the first real global culture is that which has been constructed by a West marked by the ontological error.

The salvation of the West inevitably entails its conversion, a conversion that on the philosophical level takes the form of the reception of the ontology of the Fathers, or of a critical ontology (the ontology of Greek metaphysics), and the theological and ecclesial level takes the form, rather, of a return to Christian origins, to the authenticity of the Christian experience of salvation. The two approaches are naturally not separate because salvation is none other than the realisation on the part of humanity of the authentic (true) mode of being/existing/acting and this mode of being/existing/acting is the content itself of a critical ontology.

In the earlier chapters we have examined the philosophical aspect in particular. It is now time to look at how Yannaras sees the theological/ecclesial conversion of the West. To fully understand this mode of conversion it is necessary to observe that Yannaras sets himself a problem on the strength of which the category of the 'West' undergoes a change of nature in his thinking. The problem is this: why has the West transformed the Christian experience of God in Christ and in the Church into an objective, authoritarian and inquisitional institution? In other words, why has the West stuck to the ontological error and resisted the appeals of the East?

The West in reality, by cleaving to the ontological error, has surrendered to the temptation that accompanies every human being in virtue of his or her humanity when faced with personal ontological salvation in Christ and in the Church. It is the temptation to turn faith into an ideology, to turn Christianity into a religion. The West thus becomes a historical construction extremely important for the permanent temptation of the Christian to transform the experience of salvation into a form of natural religion or into a modality that is institutional and objectively defined by humanity's self-defence when confronted by supernatural forces. This is where the heretical character of the West lies, along with the criterion for determining how much each Church is marked by heresy, because ultimately the religious distortion of Christianity is not coterminous with the West, even if it is true that historically *this* West has placed itself at the service of the religious need of individuals with the whole force of its own ontological error.

What we have said up to this point is able to explain what we shall go on to see in the rest of this chapter: first of all, the adoption by Yannaras of the Greek term *thrēskeiopoiēsē* and the meaning he develops for it in the course of the 1980s. This is an unusual term, not easily translated even if its general sense is clear enough.[1] What it indicates is the process by which an existential reality of rapport with the divine turns into an institution in the service of religious need; subsequently, it becomes a powerful appeal directed to all the churches to de-religionise themselves, an invitation to them to find again the ontological newness that constitutes the original experience of salvation in Christ and in the Church, an appeal and an invitation – one could say – to a reform of the Churches, a Eucharistic recreation of their mode of becoming in history.

2. *Thrēskeiopoiēsē*: *Religion and the Ontological Distortion of Christianity*

The term *thrēskeiopoiēsē* seems to be absent in Yannaras' writings before the 1980s. If we look carefully at works that are strongly anti-Western, such as *Alētheia kai henotēta tēs Ekklēsias* of 1977 and *Hē eleutheria tou*

---

1. The precise equivalent in English would be 'religionisation', a neologism which will be used occasionally below.

ēthous, both in the edition of 1970 and in that of 1979, we will not find this term. The terms on which Yannaras relies for his understanding of the Western alteration of Christianity are *hairesē* (heresy), *ekkosmikeusē* (secularisation) and *thesmopoiēsē* (institutionalisation). The West is an ontological heresy that reifies whatever it touches, that transforms it into a secular reality, into an objective structure, into an institution, until it alters the truth of the Church and its liturgical sense and understanding of revelation.[2] The expression closest to the meaning of *thrēskeiopoiēsē* is perhaps the one that we find in *Hē eleutheria tou* ēthous, where in discussing religious art Yannaras speaks of 'the "religious" alienation of ecclesial truth'.[3]

The first time, so far as I am aware, that we meet this word is in a volume in which Yannaras draws on a diary which he wrote during the time he spent in Moscow and Leningrad in May 1982.[4] The occasion for using it was offered by Yannaras' attendance at a concert given by Moscow's Symphony State Orchestra where some Russian religious music was performed. Yannaras reflects on this music, which seems religious but not 'ecclesial':

> I think [he writes] that the difference between orthodoxy and heresy is not an ideological difference, so even the violation of dogmatic formulations can only have a relative importance. Heresy is the appropriation in actual experience (*biomatikē oikeiōsē*) of a different concept of life and of truth, another mode of gift of the sense of life. . . . The great heresy of Christianity, the only one that has persisted throughout the centuries, is its *thrēskeiopoiēsē* in Western Europe.[5]

---

2. Cf. Yannaras, *Alētheia kai henotēta tēs Ekklēsias*, p. 128.
3. Yannaras, *Hē eleutheria tou* ēthous, 1979 edn, p. 306. In *Alphabētari tēs pistēs* [A primer of faith] (Athens: Domos, 1983), Yannaras dedicates several pages to 'religious alienation', seeing it as arising in Christian history especially at the time that Christianity becomes the 'official religion' of the Roman Empire. (There is an English translation of *Alphabētari tēs pistēs*, *Elements of Faith: An Introduction to Orthodox Theology* [Edinburgh: T. & T. Clark, 1991]). We read on p. 216 (Eng. trans., p. 145): 'To the extent that people (clergy and lay) submit the truth of the Church to our natural need for "religion" – the metaphysical self-assurance of our individuality – the Church appears in history subject to the intentionality of the religious "institution", to the mindset of "authority" and of "efficiency", to the myopic pursuits of social ethics or of the politics of the moment.'
4. I refer to Yannaras, *Hē kokkinē plateia kai ho theios Arthouros*, which, however, only appeared in 1986. It seems that the publisher was rather unwilling to publish it.
5. Ibid., p. 90.

This heresy – 'the heresy of the West'[6] – may be seen expressed with particular clarity in Western-type religious art:

> This religious art is directed towards the individual; it wants to delight the senses of the individual to suggest and stimulate the feelings of the individual . . . it is a function of power . . . it obliges one to recognise objectively the prestige and the value of the institutions or of truth that are given and infallible. . . . Under this imposition of power the religious individual finds protection and safety: He does not have to take any risk in order to arrive at participation in the knowledge of truth and of life; all is given with infallible formulations, with rules of validity endowed with authority, which reassure the ego and the individual's peace of mind.[7]

It should be noted that these reflections are offered by Yannaras on the basis of his observation of a Western presence in Russian religious art and it leads him to think that the West and Orthodox Russia in a strange way coincide: both, though each in a different way, have sought to distance themselves from the Greek prototype, differentiating themselves from it.

> All these differentiations have a common characteristic: they tend towards the pompous and the Baroque, that which works on the feelings. This concerns not a local style, but rather a different *ethos*; I would say: an *ethos* that is intensely 'religious'. The distancing from the Greco-Early Christian prototype has led imperceptibly to a western *thrēskeiopoiēsē*. If I know a little history, it was by the same need of differentiation – dictated by an anti-Greek political aim – that the Franks were moved to bring about the schism of the eleventh century.[8]

If these words were really written in 1982 (even if published in 1986) they constitute the first formulation in terms of *thrēskeiopoiēsē* of the idea of the distortion of the original Christian event on the part of

---

6. Ibid., p. 91.
7. Ibid.
8. Ibid., p. 93. In *Alphabētari tēs pistēs*, too – a volume published in 1983 – the term is used to indicate the ecclesiastical transformation that is expressed in exemplary fashion in the twelfth century's transition to gothic and the post-Byzantine Italian art of the thirteenth century (p. 234; the Eng. trans., at p. 157, simply paraphrases the term).

Western Christianity, an idea that Yannaras derived, as we have seen, from Heidegger's *Holzwege*. One should therefore not be surprised by what follows.

Nineteen eighty-six was not only the year in which Yannaras finally published the Russian diary he wrote in 1982; it was also the year he signed the preface of the second revised edition of *The Theology of the Absence and Unknowability of God*.[9] This is an interesting edition from our point of view: it is actually at this point that the term *thrēskeiopoiēsē* appears *ex novo*; and it appears precisely in a comment on the texts from Heidegger's *Holzwege* that we have just noted.

> The way in which Heidegger [writes Yannaras] understands the Nietzschean proclamation of the 'death of God' presupposes a fundamental historic testimony: the differentiation of the religionised (*thrēskeiopoiēmenou*) Christianity of the Western European tradition from the primordial fact of the experience and witness of the Church.[10]

According to Heidegger's reading:

> Nietzsche's proclamation points out, indirectly but quite clearly, the fundamental 'heresy' – the deviation from the original fact of the Church – which constitutes the historical temptation of Western Christianity: the quest to impose itself rationally and socially, finally the Church's 'religionisation', its transformation into a religion that satisfies individual needs for emotional and intellectual security, while also sustaining the practical moral interests of society.[11]

Therefore, from 1986 the word *thrēskeiopoiēsē* seems to be decisively present in Yannaras' writings. It becomes the compendious expression for defining the ontological and existential heresy of the West, the distortion of the original Christian event, which signifies that every trace of *thrēskeiopoiēsē* of whatever kind or wherever it may be found (theology, ecclesiology, ethics, sacramental theology, the various forms of art . . .) becomes a sign of Westernisation or a Western influence.

---

9. Published by Domos in 1988.
10. Yannaras, *Heidegger kai Areopagitēs: Hē theologia tēs apousias kai agnōsias tou Theou*, p. 56 (Eng. trans., p. 49).
11. Ibid., p. 53 (Eng. trans., p. 46).

Yannaras' preference for this term during the 1990s is also demonstrated by a curious fact. When, in his memoirs, he reviews *To pragmatiko kai to phantasiōdes stēn politikē oikonomia* he uses the word *thrēskeiopoiēsē* as a key term even though we do not find it in the text of 1989.[12]

In the 1990s Yannaras then published a very consistent work which uses the term – the idea and the scheme which it expresses – as part of its fundamental structure in order to present a rereading of the entire cultural history of modern Hellenism; this is *Orthodoxy and the West*, a work much discussed and in many ways highly provocative.

'The West's innovations,' writes Yannaras, 'tend towards and are summarised in a fact which we may call "religionisation" of the Church.' Christianity is a mode of ecclesial and eucharistic existence: this mode was well and truly lost in the West, where 'Christianity came to be transformed into an individual "*thrēskeia*", into an ideology of individual convictions, into a morality of individual merit and into an institutional organisation objective control of the convictions and morality of individuals'.[13]

Yannaras goes on to say:

> In reality Western Christianity represents within history the radical reversal of the terms of the Christian Gospel. Step by step, alongside each particular affirmation and formulation of ecclesial experience one can set the corresponding Western novelty, the undisguised distortion and corruption of the Gospel kerygma. The axis and recapitulation of the alterations is the *thrēskeiopoiēsē* of the ecclesial event: the West rejects (or fails to understand) the priority of the truth of the person; it returns to the abstract intellectual conception of God as supreme Essence.[14]

In successive years of the 1990s and the first years of the new millennium, it would be easy to demonstrate the significant presence of the term.[15] Nevertheless, it seems to me more important to underline a significant modification of the notion of the West that is associated with this term.

---

12. Yannaras, *Ta kath' eauton*, p. 143.
13. Yannaras, *Orthodoxia kai Dysē stē neōterē Hellada*, p. 44 (Cf. Eng. trans., pp. 23, 24).
14. Ibid., p. 56 (Cf. Eng. trans., p. 33).
15. Cf. Christos Yannaras, *Hē apanthrōpia tou dikaiōmatos* (The inhumanity of right) (Athens: Domos, 1998), pp. 138, 141, 148, 228; Yannaras, *To rhēto kai to arrhēto*, p. 313, where Yannaras speaks of 'the twin *thrēskeiopoiēsē* (Catholic and Protestant) of the ecclesial event'; Yannaras, *Kommatokratia*, pp. 131, 138, 245-48, 250.

Yannaras gives increasing attention to the fact that *thrēskeiopoiēsē* constitutes the victory of natural religion over the experience of salvation in the Church, over the ecclesial event: natural religion is the system of collective convictions, of rites and moral rules that flow from the need of human beings to protect and safeguard themselves with regard to transcendent forces.[16] In consequence the dualism is shifted, or, better expressed, the West-East dualism comes to be grafted on to a dualism that is broader and more radical: the dualism between *thrēskeiopoiēsē* and ecclesial event, or rather, between *thrēskeia* and ecclesial event, as emerges very clearly in *Enantia stē thrēskeia* (Against religion).[17]

This does not signify the complete loss of the primacy of ontological Hellenism, nor does it change the ontological interpretation of the Schism; it nevertheless signifies the Western *thrēskeiopoiēsē* (in the form twinned with Protestantism) is only one of the forms of *thrēskeiopoiēsē*: there also exists an Eastern form of it (Orthodoxism), partly determined by Western influence after the Schism (scholastic and confessional theology, art), but also partly derived directly from the imperial Church (certain Sacred Canons, for example, and the role of the Sacred Canons in general), and partly generated from within. Yannaras, as we shall see, is strongly critical of Philokalian hesychasm.

Nevertheless, 'the ultimate stage of *thrēskeiopoiēsē* even of the so-called Orthodox Churches'[18] does not lie in these aspects but in the fact that the Churches continue to give credit to a cosmology and a mythological anthropology (the prelapsarian world of myth) that are incompatible with the findings of modern science without in any way treating such a dualism as a problem. For Yannaras the Orthodox Churches seem to accept becoming a place of psychological refuge in a mythical world that corresponds to humanity's desires and instinctual needs and is almost a projection of them.

This modification of the sense of the term of *thrēskeiopoiēsē* has a particular effect: the ontological difference between East and West comes to be based on a more primary difference, anthropological rather than ontological, a difference between the person who tries to enclose the Gospel message within the limits of natural religion and the person who accepts the evangelical (ecclesial) transformation of the mode of existence, a new mode of existence that nevertheless maintains aspects of continuity with the Greek mode of existence that was realised in an exemplary fashion in the first Christian centuries.

---

16. Cf. Yannaras, *Ontologia tēs scheseōs*, pp. 151-61 (Eng. trans., pp. 80-87).
17. Athens: Ikaros, 2006.
18. Yannaras, *Enantia stē thrēskeia*, p. 271 (Eng. trans., p. 173).

This difference exists not only between one person and another, but also between the individual person and the community: *thrēskeiopoiēsē* is the constant temptation that accompanies the very message of the Gospel and its reception: like the wheat and the tares, so *thrēskeiopoiēsē* and the Gospel message grow together until the moment of harvest.[19]

That does not affect the ontological significance of Hellenism and does not diminish Yannaras' conviction that Hellenism has attempted heroically to oppose the religious transformation of Christianity, but without success.[20]

One can thus say that the term 'West' in Yannaras' current thinking has a more general meaning that is the surrender of the Christian to the temptation to transform the Gospel message into a natural religion instead of assuming the natural religious need and transforming it in the eucharistic experience, in the ecclesial mode of existence. This temptation has found in the historical West a profound success of its own but it is fully active everywhere and in all periods, not excluding the Orthodox Churches.

From what I have just said it would appear that for Yannaras natural religion cannot simply be negated; it has to be assumed and transformed. Just as the sacrament of matrimony assumes and transforms the sexual need because it grafts it on to the ecclesial mode of existence, and just as the Eucharist grafts on to the same mode the need of self-preservation, so the natural religious need of human beings can be assumed and transformed in the very event of the Church, in the sacrament that the Church itself is as:

> a realisation and manifestation of the Triadic mode of existence. This mode is realised and manifested by the synaxis of the 'body' of the Church in every particular sacramental act, above all, however, in the supper of the Eucharist, where the realisation and manifestation of the body is accomplished by active participation in eating and drinking of the one bread and the one cup.[21]

Human beings, in this perspective, can withdraw themselves from the circle of imprisonment in natural religion only if they accept the

---

19. Yannaras, *To ainigma tou kakou*, p. 123 (Eng. trans., p. 61).
20. Ibid., p. 157 (Eng. trans., p. 79): 'One could say that resistance to the "religionisation" of the fact of the Church came to an end historically with the Fall of Constantinople. From that time onward the universal entrapment of the life of Christians in the mode of the created, in the necessity for individualism, seems to have become an irreversible process: an inexplicable limitation of human freedom, a historical consolidation of evil.'
21. Yannaras, *Enantia stē thrēskeia*, p. 313 (Eng. trans., p. 201).

ontological call to Trinitarian existence. I leave aside here the fact that this final perspective stimulates Yannaras to a reassessment of original sin, something which he attempts specifically in *Ontologia tēs scheseōs*.

3. Against Religion: *Natural Religion, the Religious Transformation of Christianity and the Reform of the Church*

Enantia stē thrēskeia (Against religion) is a rather unusual work, as already appears from the choice of the title, in which all the ferments of Yannaras' thought condense into a claim of Christian novelty irreducible to any institutionalisation of a religious type. For the Greek theologian the religious instinct is innate in human beings and is part of the way their natural existence functions. It allows them to overcome fear, to organise the cosmos in which they live in a way that is controllable and comprehensible and it offers dogmatic certainties and a sacred and solid hierarchy. The religious instinct is a need of the individual of the human species and is orientated towards the reinforcement of the individual. Christianity is born and manifests itself as an existential event which has a different direction, not the empowerment of the individual and the safeguarding of his natural needs but the realisation of the personal truth of human existence in freedom from nature, in sharing and in love. Christianity is a new mode of existence in communion, according to the intimate and radical Trinitarian truth of Man made in the image and likeness of God.

From the beginnings of Christianity, however, the religious instinct has sought to take it over, to make a religious institution of it and in large measure it has succeeded. The symptoms of this institutionalisation are evident: faith as ideology; the experience of salvation as a psychological fact; salvation as the result of individual merit; the eucharistic assembly as a sacred rite; art enslaved to impressions; the eclipse of the parish; the idolatry of tradition; the demonisation of sexuality.

So then, this success of the religious instinct has become particularly visible in Western Christianity from the time of St Augustine. However, Orthodoxy too has surrendered to it – has become in some way Western, Orthodoxism, as Yannaras calls it, meaning by this term the transformation of Orthodoxy-Church into Orthodoxy-religion. He claims to be able to show as manifest proof of such a success of 'religion' even in the East itself the incredible Western success of the *Philokalia* – not so incredible, he notes, if one considers its individualistic stamp: the West may be recognised in it:

> We Orthodox [writes Yannaras] like to accuse the West of institutional rigidity and of imposing religionisation on the

ecclesial event, of submitting it to intellectualism, moralism and legalism. But the case of the *Philokalia* proves rather that the West is 'within us' – its historical outgrowths dwell in an obscure way in the 'inward' instinctive need of every human being for individualistic self-protection and assurance. The ego likes to be self-sufficient. The urge for autonomy is built into our nature (is an existential presupposition). We want the provenance of faith, of knowledge and of salvation to come from within us, to be our own achievement. Hence the historically decisive change of direction with Augustine from eucharistic participation to the 'interiority' and 'spirituality' of the individual (in a closed self-referential autarky) is repeated as the supreme realisation of Christian authenticity in every age.[22]

Therefore, the West becomes a negative category of a moral type that serves to designate the permanent temptation of the naturally religious human being to appropriate salvation by making it his own achievement instead of opening himself to the event of communion and of freedom made possible in the Church.

This (im)moral reading of the West may surprise readers and perhaps also scandalise them. In Yannaras' intellectual journey, however, it also signifies a judgement on contemporary Orthodoxy, or rather is the presentation of a line of reform of the Church which, beyond the historical vicissitudes and classifications of fidelity, concerns both Churches, the Catholic as well as the Orthodox; both in reality have need of conversion and of becoming again an event of new existence, the actualisation of the manifestation in history of the mode of being of God, an infinite experience of freedom in an inexhaustible communion of love.

---

22. Ibid., p. 304 (Eng. trans., p. 196).

Epilogue

The journey we have undertaken has demonstrated – I hope – a clear continuity of research and thinking in Christos Yannaras. Indeed, in the distinction of the phases which he himself has several times delineated and the various successive discoveries that have allowed him to express his own reflection ever more amply and deeply, Yannaras has explored the historical, cultural and existential differences between East and West, finding in the Hellenisation of Christianity and the Christianisation of Hellenism the place of the adequate manifestation – on the cognitive and existential levels – of the authenticity of Christian experience and at the same time the way out of the nihilistic *impasse* that Western ontological thinking has been taken into, founded as it also is on an imperfect reading of Greek philosophical thought.

The meeting between Hellenism and Christianity has been able to take place without substantial gnoseological discontinuity because Hellenism has persevered in the knowledge of truth as the truth of existence, in the apophatic awareness of the way existence goes beyond concepts and rational notions, offering, as a way of verifying affirmations on existence, the way of placing-in-common, the way of communality.

The Christian novelty of creation as an act of freedom by a free God is grafted on to this apophatic gnoseological base, modifying the deterministic ontology of the Greeks but without a break as regards their gnoseological approach. Thus, in some way, one can say that the Greek gnoseological approach finds in the Christian ontological novelty (the mystery of the Triune God) an adequate foundation, since the free person hypostasises nature or essence, and being is resolved into relation.

Christos Yannaras
The Communal Verification of Knowledge[1]

[A note by Basilio Petrà: The following text is a translation of the first chapter of Christos Yannaras, *Exi philosophikes zōgraphies: 'Ekomisa eis tēn technēn'* (Athens: Ikaros, 2011), pp. 15-48. (The English translation has been made directly from the Greek.) As the title of the volume suggests, this chapter is the first philosophical picture; it is the first, that is to say, of the paintings in the philosophical gallery exhibited by Yannaras. In each of these pictures he assembles themes that are fully present in his preceding works, which, moreover, are cited in the notes. This explains why it has its own coherent autonomy, yet is also intimately connected with the rest of his *oeuvre*. The notes, unless otherwise indicated, are Yannaras' own.]

---

1. [The Greek title is: '*Hē koinōnikē epalētheusē tēs gnōsēs*'. On the choice of the language of communality, Cf. my remarks on p. 22, note 24 above, where the work containing this essay is cited. Basilio Petrà's note.]

1. The Genesis of Critical Thought

Critical thought, as we call it today, was born for the first time in human history six or seven centuries BC on the shores of the Aegean. What was born was the need of the Greeks to distinguish the real from the illusory, truth from falsehood, valid knowledge from subjective impression or opinion, the need to distinguish discourse that was worthy of credence (*pistos*) from discourse that was unworthy (*apistos*). Philosophy was born, scientific thought.

Both critical thought and the vehicle of its expression, language, emerged from a collective need – they were not the creations of particular, charismatic individuals. Language, and all that it expresses as a mode (*tropos*) of thought, is the fruit of a common (shared) need. The common need generates the codes that are required for mutual understanding (*syn-ennoēsē*). Critical thought emerged as a demand of the Greeks that in their collective life truth should have priority over utility.

The priority of utility in the collective life (the sharing of need) is a natural mark of human existence: *physei* (by nature, by necessity) a human being is a *zōon koinōnikon* (a social animal, or an animal that lives in communion with others). By the division of labour and relations of exchange, the needs vital for life are shared, an organised collectivity is constituted. The axis of cohesion is a necessary utilitarianism.

At some stage there arose for the Greeks, as a primary need, the demand for truth. The goal of the collectivity became the sharing of truth. Need was not ignored or despised. It was simply the priorities that changed. The common and self-evident priority for the Greeks was the need that life should be true, that existence and the coexistence of human beings should be in accordance with truth.[2]

It is very clear that the priority of truth emerged as a common need. It was not a moral commandment or an idealistic demand. It was a primary need, that is to say, a more urgent need than those which were utilitarian and it was a common need, a need that was shared experientially. It was the fruit of the mode of mutual understanding (*syn-ennoēsē*), of a common prioritisation of needs, of common goals.

The first appearance in human history of critical thought was formulated in the *fragmenta* of written texts of the pre-Socratic Greek philosophers. They are historically the first examples of philosophy, of epistemic thought. They date from the sixth century BC.

---

2. Cf. *Schediasma eisagogēs stē philosophia*, §§ 13, 16 (Eng. trans., pp. 43-46, 59-64); *Orthos logos kai koinōnikē praktikē*, V 1a; Protaseis *Kritikēs Ontologias*, §§ 2, 2.12.

* * *

We have defined critical thought as a need and a mode by which we judge and distinguish (*dia-krinoume, xechorizoume*) what is true and what is false, what is correct and what is mistaken, what is real and what is illusory – which information of the individual senses or which concept of the individual mind constitutes valid knowledge and which constitutes non-valid knowledge.

This collective need was born among the Greeks as a demand for the priority of truth rather than of necessity, but it is not everywhere and always that the need for validity has not been subordinated to utility. In medieval and modern Europe (in the West to the present day) the mode of the critical thought of the Greeks was adopted with enthusiasm, but for its utilitarian value[3] – it was transformed into a need for efficacy, which is the most impudent manifestation of utilitarianism. That is why even scientific knowledge, which has been cultivated with impressive results in the West, serves the priority of utility in a very consistent manner, even if it concerns the utility of Auschwitz or Hiroshima.

In the Greek case the rise of critical thought was preserved without its being subordinated to utilitarianism (thus creating a civilisation at the opposite pole to that of modern and contemporary Western Europe), because it was linked from its origins to the need for truth to be determined not simply as knowledge but also as existence. This determination proved to be necessary also because it came to be specified as a criterion of the functioning of critical thought – a criterion of the distinction of the correct from the mistaken, of the true from the false.

Wherever critical thought has been subjected to utilitarianism, the criterion of truth (the criterion of correctness, of validity) has been sought in its useful result – or in more general principles of utilitarian efficacy, such as the principle of authority, the principle of the majority, the principle of irrefutable proof, the principle of advantageous contract.[4] That is to say, an attestation, an opinion, an item of information is judged as correct and valid if it has a useful result – or if its correctness is guaranteed by a commonly acknowledged authority or by the majority of members of a collectivity, or if it is accompanied by irrefutable proofs, or if it is imposed by a contract ('by convention', by common agreement) by the will of the majority. From its genesis (around the sixth century

---

3. Cf. *Schediasma eisagōges stē philosophia*, Ch. 3 (Eng. trans., pp. 21-30); *Hē apanthrōpia tou dikaiōmatos*, III, § 4; *Orthos logos kai koinōnike praktikē*, II, 2a.
4. *Schediasma eisagōges stē philosophia*, Ch. 3, § 19 (Eng. trans., pp. 87-95); *To pragmatiko kai to phantasiōdes stēn politikē oikonomia*, 5b, 9c.

AD) to our own day, post-Roman Europe has been trapped, with no means of escape, in the search for an 'objective' criterion of truth that will guarantee absolute certainty to the individual. The absolutisation of the demand for subjective certainty through guarantees of absolute objectivity is the Sisyphean demand (or the historical schizophrenia) of Western European culture, a culture that has inverted the terms of that of ancient Greece.

2. Truth as Mode

In the case of the Greeks the criterion of critical thought (the presupposition of the indication of truth) was sought originally not in an 'objective' guarantor of the correctness of knowledge but in identifying the mode of existence 'in accordance with truth'. The Greeks clearly asked themselves: what datum of reality exists 'truly', that is, without limitations to its existence, limitations of space, time, decay, transformation and change, or death? That which really exists, which is without presuppositions and eternal (*to ontōs on*), is, self-evidently, a criterion of truth. The mode by which it is constitutes the measure of existence in accordance with truth, and thus also knowledge in accordance with truth.

The Greeks identified this mode of truth with the given rationality of the universe, with the *logos xynos* (*xyn-nooi*: in accordance with the mind of all, the common mind) a *logos* that defines the existence and the coexistence of the totality of existents, that manifests the reality of the universe as *kosmos*, which means an ornament (*kosmēma*). It is the *logos*-mode[5] of the essence of every existent (the how of its participation

---

5. [The author uses the expression *logos-tropos*: it has been decided to keep the Greek form *logos* and to translate *tropos* by the English word mode. The reason for this decision is that, whereas mode corresponds reasonably well to the Greek *tropos*, though it should be borne in mind that the Greek term – which derives from the stem of the verb *trepō* (I change) – has a more dynamic character, the term *logos* has a semantic range that no English word can cover. In particular, in Yannaras' thought, as he himself says in *Protaseis kritikēs ontologias*, s. 1.3: 'The Greek term *logos* signifies-signals every event of manifestation – the appearance of the signifier is always a *logos* declarative of a presence. That something is signified means: something declares itself to be present, something says to us "I am here." The signifier is always referential; it represents something for someone and the only mode of reference that we know is the mode of *logos*.' Therefore the content of the Greek word in English is expressed by 'signified', 'form' or 'reason': '*Logos* is what is signified in oral discourse (the sounds and their articulation in "acoustic images"); *logos* is the inherent sense that accompanies every acoustic image; *logos* is

in being). It shapes the individual form of existents and their formation as a totality. It constitutes the eternal rational order, harmony, beauty (*kosmiotēta*) of the *kosmos*.⁶

The common (*xynos*) *logos* precedes existence and defines it – it predetermines any existence, even that of divinity. The gods or God are that which necessity imposes: the rational necessity to be causes of, and administrators of, the becoming of the cosmos or to be the one unique cause of universal beauty (*kosmiotēs*), the first mover, the most noble race, supreme being.⁷

* * *

In reality the (eternal and immutable) mode of the existence and of the coexistence of existents, the rationality of *eidē* (forms) and the relation between them is the standard or criterion of verification and of knowledge. Knowledge (attestation, opinion, information) is true (is correct, valid, worthy of credence) when it is in accordance with *logos* (*kata logon*) and rationally organised (*ana ton logon*): it echoes, imitates, reproduces relations in a harmony of co-understanding (*syn-ennoēsē*), of the rational coordination of the functioning of the intellect and the experience of single individuals.

Human beings are rational not because they have a mind (*nous* – the capacity of intellection) but because with this capacity they can come to a common mind (*syn-ennoeitai*), can put together rational relations communicating their experience. We become rational by participation, says Heraclitus,⁸ that is, in the degree in which by our intellectual capacity we participate in the mode of the arrangement of the whole, the mode of the common (*xynou*) *logos*: in the rational harmony of relations.⁹

---

    the form (the *eidos* or species) of every sensible object in so far as the form signifies it (makes it accessible to "seeing", to immediate vision); *logos* is every total configuration (structure, articulation, harmonious order) that signifies a state of things different from other states of things' (ibid., s. 1.31). Basilio Petrà's note.]

6. *Schediasma eisagōgēs stē philosophia*, § 13 (Eng. trans., pp. 43-46); *Metaneōterikē meta-physikē*, Thesis 1 and Thesis 2 (Eng. trans., pp. 83-170); *To prosōpo kai ho erōs*, § 24 (Eng. trans., pp. 73-75).
7. 'Everything is from *logos* and by necessity' (Leucippus, Diels-Kranz, *Die Fragmente der Vorsokratiker*, vol. 2, 81.5); 'All things become by necessity and harmony' (Philolaus, Diels-Kranz, *Die Fragmente der Vorsokratiker*, vol. 1, 398. 11); 'It is necessary that there should be a first mover that is one and eternal' (Aristotle, *Physics*, 8.6, 259a14); *To prosōpo kai ho erōs*, § 20 (Eng. trans., pp.55-59).
8. Diels-Kranz, *Die Fragmente der Vorsokratiker*, vol. 1, 148.21.
9. Ibid., 148.28-29.

Attestation, opinion, information are true when they provoke and form rational relations of common co-understanding, when they coordinate (harmonise) particular (individual) experiences, when they allow the experience to be held in common: 'In so far as we share in common, we say what is true,' says Heraclitus, 'but when we express our private thoughts, we say what is false.'[10]

What precisely does 'sharing experience in common' mean? Democritus offers an interpretative example: if someone expresses the attestation-information-opinion that 'honey is sour', his *logos* is not coordinated (does not *sym-phōnei*, does not *homo-phōnei*) with the experience of all who have tasted honey. This person *idiazei* (expresses his private thought), he has his *idian* (his own private and personal) opinion-point of view; his witness is outside the common *logos* of the experience of his fellow human beings. He is saying what is false not because he is opposing, denying or transgressing some 'principle' (authority, majority, demonstrative method, convention) that defines what is sweet and what is sour. He says what is false because the *logos* of his testimony is not participated, does not refer to an experience that can be shared by all; his *logos* is not held in common.[11] What is false is testimony-opinion-information that cannot be shared empirically (that is not communicable); it is what is strictly individual, a private thought or idea. Conversely, what is true (correct, valid, trustworthy) is that which all hold in common (*pantes homodoxousin*) as a common opinion (*doxa-gnomē*) and to which each (from his own individual experience) testifies (*epimartyrei*).

3. Correct Thinking (Orthōs Dianoeisthai) through Correctly Sharing in Common (Orthōs Koinōnein)

It is insufficient to say that the Greeks set their mark on human history because they gave birth to critical thought (the rational method, demonstrative cohesiveness). What sets its mark on history is that which liberates humanity from its subjection to the inexorable law of the instincts, and critical thought on its own can still be tapped within the necessity of the instinctual urges of self-interest, the primitiveness of

---

10. Ibid., 148.29-30. [Yannaras cites here a passage found in Sextus Empiricus (*Adversus Mathematicos*, 7, 133 or *Against the Logicians*, 1, 133) that Sextus refers to the doctrine of Heraclitus. It is variously translated. The translation of R.G. Bury in the Loeb edition of Sextus Empiricus (vol. 2, 73-75) is as follows: 'Therefore in so far as we share in the memory of that reason we say what is true, but whenever we utter our own private thoughts, we lie.' Basilio Petrà's note.]
11. Diels-Kranz, *Die Fragmente der Vorsokratiker*, vol. 2, 119.22-26.

utilitarianism. The awareness of this testimony is reflected in Aristotle's dictum: 'To be always seeking after the useful does not become free and exalted souls.'[12] The supreme architect of the rational method sets the absolutisation of utility against the pursuit of freedom and magnanimity.

The Greeks set their mark on human history because they based the critical functioning of thought on the primacy of the communal event, on the effort to attain freedom, which for the Greeks was the *polis* (city-state), the political life of the collectivity. The criterion for critical functioning of thought (for distinguishing what is correct from what is mistaken, truth from falsehood) was the communal verification of knowledge: 'In so far as we hold in common, we say what is true; but when we express our private thoughts, we say what is false.'

The rational method, the techniques of demonstrative proof, which the Greeks first introduced, are not the mode of the verification of knowledge, the sufficient means, the instrument or *organon* of verification. Rational method and techniques of demonstrative proof function as presuppositions of thinking correctly, which serves and assures communicating correctly. The correctness of thinking refers to the integrity of the method, of the mode of articulating thought (and consequently of language) – without this correctness, common understanding, the intelligible (*kata-noētos*, that is, *kata-ton-noun*, in accordance-with-the-mind of all) mode of the declaration (manifestation) of experience, would be unattainable; the sharing of experience would elude us. Ultimately, however, knowledge is verified by the holding of experience in common, not by the correctness of the process of thinking (individually), even if thinking correctly is presupposed in order for holding in common correctly to be able to function.

The guarantee of truth is that knowledge should be held in common, that individual experiences should be coordinated rationally (*kata logon* – in accordance with *logos*). This rational coordination is served by the method and techniques of demonstrative proof, and before these by language, the linguistic code of common understanding. The criterion of truth is the rational communication of experience, the attainment of relations of communion. The rational method alone, or the common sharing of need alone, do not guarantee truth – critical thought, simply as a technical tool, shapes a mode of common life (history and culture) that inverts the Greek terms.[13]

---

12. *Politics*, 8.3, 1338b2-4 (Oxford trans.); *Hē apanthrōpia tou dikaiomatos*, Ch. 3, b, 3 (pp. 38-40).
13. *Orthos logos kai koinōnikē praktikē*, 5.1; *Meta-neōterikē meta-physikē*, Prolegomena 1.3, Thesis 1.1 (Eng. trans., pp. 7-11, 83-97).

4. A Shared Empiricism

The criterion of the communal verification of knowledge bases gnoseology, the theory of knowledge, on a thoroughly coherent empiricism: it excludes any recourse to *a priori* truths, imposed dogmas, accepted axiomatic principles.

Empiricism, in the Greek case, again means freedom from the individual's epistemic powers (which tend towards self-interest): information from the individual senses, conceptions of the individual understanding, products of individual perception, the 'existential' experiences of the individual. Empiricism is not the primacy of nature (potentiality), but the primacy of relation (freedom): the volitional-energetic inclusion of all the natural epistemic potentialities in the actualisation – free from natural needs – of relation. That is why the fullest knowledge, as Plato says, is *erōs*:[14] the relation which arrives at freedom from any self-interest, at self-offering.

Moreover, an empiricism shut up in the cognitive potentialities of the individual inevitably destroys itself: it generates (in a wholly consistent manner) the need for an 'objective' reinforcement of subjective experience, that is to say, a recourse to an extra-experiential factor capable of making the subjective experience obligatory for all. By contrast, the empiricism of the Greek theory of knowledge is the empiricism of relation: of free participation in the common *logos* by which knowledge is shared. It is the attainment of withdrawing from living for oneself (*idiazein*), the attainment freedom from self-interest.

* * *

The empiricism of the Greeks brings with it a respect for the otherness (the uniqueness, dissimilarity) of every individual experience, and consequently the acceptance of the relativity of every opinion-attestation-information that is expressed (signified by a code of common usage and objective semantic content). For the Greeks the difference between the signifiers and the signified is always a given, both in the denotation-signification of empirical knowledge and in the experience of knowledge itself. The signifiers allow us to share the reference to experience, but they cannot be substituted for cognitive experience.[15]

---

14. *Symposium*, 204-05, 207-11; *Republic*, 6, 499c2; *Laws*, 4, 711d6.
15. Cf. *To rhēto kai to arrhēto*, chapters 1-5; *Protaseis kritikēs ontologies*, ss. 2.22, 2.3, 2.321, 2.331; *To prosōpo kai ho erōs*, § 61 (Eng. trans., pp. 173-76); *To pragmatiko kai to phantasiōdes stēn politikē oikonomia*, pp. 40-42.

This obvious difference functions only in the case of the empiricism of the Greeks when the criterion of the critical functioning of thought is the communal verification of knowledge. In that case correct and valid knowledge is not identified either with individual comprehension of the signifiers of common experience alone. The distance between the signifiers of knowledge and the knowledge that is signified is only transcended by the accord (*syntonismos*) or communion (*koinonia*) between individual experience and common experience.

(Someone who has never tasted honey in his life certainly comprehends the sentence: 'honey is sweet', but he does not know the particular sweetness of honey – he does not participate empirically in the knowledge that is signified, does not share [*koinonei*] in the truth of the expression. Another person, who has tasted honey and knows its sweetness but declares that 'honey is sour', violates the code of common semantics and for this reason does not communicate his experience either, invalidating its verification and experiencing reality as an individual illusion.)

5. Symbol

The signifying-formulation of cognitive experience by the common linguistic code of com-prehension (*syn-ennoēsē*) or by the 'languages' of humanity's capacity for poetry, the languages of the various arts, presupposes that the code should function symbolically. The Greek word *symbolo* comes from the verb *symballō* (*syn* + *ballō*) which means: I put together, I coordinate, I harmonise. The function of language is for the Greeks always symbolic; the words – the names (*onomata*) by which we name things (*pragmata*, things in the sense of that which has been made or done) or goods (*chrēmata*, objects of use) – function as symbols. 'There is nothing that belongs to names by nature, but only when they become symbols,' says Aristotle.[16] That is to say, by their nature names as spoken sounds are nothing; they signify nothing, they refer to nothing. They are (they become something) when they function as symbols, when they *syn-balloun*, put together, bring into accord, particular individual experiences and provoke com-prehension (*syn-ennoēsē*).

An example: for a non-Greek speaker the Greek word *potami* (river) is simply a phoneme without meaning; it signifies nothing. For a Greek speaker, however, the same phoneme evokes images-representations-

---

16. *Sophistical Refutations*, 165a 7-8; *De Interpretatione*, 16a 27-28. Cf. also *Schediasma eisagōgēs stē philosophia*, § 8 (Eng. trans., pp. 23-26); *To prosōpo kai ho erōs*, §§ 56, pp. 58-59 (Eng. trans., pp. 159-63, 165-70); *Protaseis kritikēs ontologias*, 2.13, 2.14; *To rhēto kai to arrhēto*, pp. 35-40.

associations-feelings (the cognitive experience) of as many rivers as he has seen in his life. And the recollection of cognitive experience evoked by the phoneme is not the accumulation of images of all the particular rivers that the subject has ever seen, but is the result of a critical activity, a process of abstraction that the mind exercises on the empirical matter of all the relevant images: the mind abstracts all the accidents from the uniform genus (*eidos*) of the existents, that is to say, all the individual properties, all the accidental, contingent and circumstantial elements, and retains in a mental image (an image that is *en-nōi*, in the mind, in Greek an *ennoia* being a concept or an idea) only the characteristics that make every river a river, every lily a lily, every deer a deer.

We call the critical function of the mind its ability to evaluate-discern the characteristics that define and differentiate the *katholou* (universal) unity of a uniform genus (*eidos*) of existents (the unity of all the existents that have the same genus or form, that have common formal characteristics). The mind retains, as a concept-idea, the characteristics of the common *logos-mode* of the participation of every *eidos* of existents in existence: it retains the *logos* of the essence (*ousia*) of every existent. This critico-abstractive function is a presupposition both of thought (the putting together of concepts, the articulation of rational propositions) and of com-prehension (*syn-ennoēsē*) (the coincidence, coordination, harmonisation of individual experiences, occasionally the common symbols).

Thus, although the individual experiences of each one of us derived from whatever rivers we have seen in our life are unique, dissimilar and unrepeatable, when we hear (or see written) the word river, we all recall the abstract *ennoia*-idea that is common to all (not private) – with the appearance or the hearing of the symbol all the concepts (*ennoies*) of each individual mind are put together (*sym-ballontai*) and comprehension occurs.[17]

Symbols, in the function of the sharing or communication of experience, are not only the words (both written and as phonemes); they are also every language in the various arts by which human experiences are signified-shared. Symbols are also the chosen figures or objects that distinguish-mark-evoke the function of the sharing of experiences of a collectivity. A flag, for example, of an organised collectivity is a symbol, just as is the escutcheon of a historic family, the uniform of state officials,

---

17. Cf. *Schediasma eisagōgēs stē philosophia*, §§ 14, 15 (Eng. trans., pp. 47-57); *To prosōpo kai ho erōs*, §§ 8, 9, 10 (Eng. trans., pp. 25-34); *Protaseis kritikēs ontologias*, pp. 58-67; *Meta-noēterikē meta-physikē*, Thesis 3 (Eng. trans., pp. 171-82).

the laurel crown of victors in games and so on. For an African of the Kikuyu tribe the French flag is perhaps only a cloth in three colours: blue, white and red. For French people, however, this cloth is the icon of their country, of its history and of its culture – this cloth makes them experience in their personal life a sense of origin and continuity, badges of dignity.

6. *Apophaticism*

From the symbolic sense of the function of language and the identification of knowledge with experiential attestation comes the gnoseological principle of apophaticism.

A gnoseological principle is a mode (method, presupposition or 'position') for controlling the validity of knowledge. It is a mode with general application in the fields of philosophy, the natural and social sciences, and the interpretation of art.

The definition of apophaticism has already been formulated in what has already been stated up to this point: it is the refusal to identify the comprehension of the signifiers with the knowledge of the signified, the refusal to exhaust knowledge in its formulation.

The definition is deduced from the two admissions that derive from experience: the symbolic version of language – that words and syntax function as symbols; and the identification of knowledge with an attestation that is chiefly experiential – where experience signifies the coordination of all the subject's cognitive powers with the event of intersubjective relation or even of the relation of the knowing subject with every object-phenomenon-happening.

* * *

The term *apophasis* (*apo* + *phēmi*), together with the term *kataphasis*, signify in ancient Greek literature modes of either negative or positive lexical attestation: *Apophasis tou einai leukon to mē einai leukon* ('The negation of "to be white" is "not to be white"').[18] We can attest to, or define, an existent by attributing to its positive characteristics (saying what it is, how it is), but we can also define it by negative characteristics (saying what it is not). By excluding positive categories (cataphatic affirmations) we gradually allow the otherness of the signified to make its appearance indirectly as its identity, without the signified being subjected to an objective definition. The cataphatic method has been compared to the way in which we form a statue out of clay by progressively adding

---

18. Aristotle, *Prior Analytics*, 1. 46, 51b 8-9.

material, and the apophatic method with the way in which we chisel a statue out of marble by gradually removing material.[19]

The second method, the apophatic one, has proved to be a particularly productive path of knowledge in cases in which the signified exists as a continuously realised otherness, not subject to a fixed definition. Such cases of the signified are the personal existence of human beings and the creations (*demiourgēmata*) – 'things made' (*poiēmata*) – on which human beings stamp the otherness of their persons. So too are the creations – 'things made' – of beauty and wisdom (reflections of the *logos* of personal otherness) that compose the nature of the universe.

This broadening of the cognitive function of *apophases* (of apophatic expressions) was achieved gradually in Hellenism's historical journey. If Heraclitus (in the sixth century BC) was the supreme exponent of the apophatic method, the *Areopagitical Writings* (in the fifth century AD) mark the culminating point of its employment. Apophatic formulations signified, in the Greek perspective, something more than a possible alternative (in relation to cataphatic formulations) mode of knowledge. They were identified with the coherent denial that we can exhaust the knowledge of the signified simply in the comprehension of the signifiers; apophatic forms of expression demonstrated the language of poetry and the visual arts of allegory and metaphor, as a way of cognition. Even in the field of the natural sciences today (in the study of sensory reality), many attestations cannot be expressed except by an apophatic semantics.[20]

7. *The Historical Eclipse of Apophaticism*

We have already said in the preceding pages that the post-Roman world that emerged after the invasion of the (principally) Germanic tribes (from the fourth to the sixth centuries) and their settlement on Roman territory never suspected, in the course of its fertile historical development, the advantages of the apophatic tradition of the Greeks, the dynamic of the criterion of the communal verification of knowledge. The need, centred on the individual, for cladding oneself in the armour of 'objective' certainties, for avoiding the risk that accompanies the

---

19. Cf. *Heidegger kai Areopagitēs*, B, 1-4 (Eng. trans., pp. 59-110); *To prosōpo kai ho erōs*, §§ 7, 58, 67 (Eng. trans., pp. 20-23, 165-67, 190-94); *Orthos logos kai koinōnikē praktikē*, 5. 1; *Schediasma eisagōgēs stē philosophia*, § 18 (Eng. trans., pp. 72-85); *To rhēto kai to arrhēto*, pp. 155-56, 256; *Ontologia tēs scheseēs*, 2.6-12 (Eng. trans., pp. 9-67).
20. Cf. *Meta-neōterikē meta-physikē*, Thesis 1a (Eng. trans., pp. 83-97); *Orthos logos kai koinōnikē praktikē*, 6. 2c; *To pragmatiko kai to phantasiōdes stēn politikē oikonomia*, 10d.

indeterminacy and relativity of the empiricism of relation, has remained the specific difference of the West, a position that does not coincide with the culture of the Greeks. Today there is no longer any collectivity that would function as the bearer of continuity with the culture of the Greeks, and consequently the attestation of its radical difference from the medieval and modern (globalised) culture of the West cannot reasonably be taken to represent a defensive nationalistic reaction or a historical habitude, rivalry or ideological competitiveness.

The apophaticism-communocentrism of the tradition of both ancient and Christianised Hellenism remains a historical exception, a measure of an acquired freedom with regard to the primitivism of the need for individually-centred certainties. Despite the boast of the post-Roman West that it is the successor and continuator of the ancient Greek tradition of philosophy and science, the denial of the fundamental characteristics of Hellenism, of apophaticism and of communocentrism, does not allow any margin of reality for this boast. Certainly, the West has produced a paradigm of utilitarianism with astonishing results, but clearly this relates to a culture that has inverted the Greek terms.

It is characteristic that, when the barbarian West in its medieval youth discovered with enthusiasm Aristotle's 'thinking correctly' detached from its aim, 'so as to share correctly', the West became trapped in an instrumental, utilitarian version of the Aristotelian rational method, and took it to be an *organon* (instrument) of an authoritative efficacy. There followed, as a consistent progeny, an enthusiastic faith in sensism, always with a utilitarian aim. Sensism was succeeded by faith in the rationality of nature turned into an efficacious instrument, faith in the triad observation-experiment-mathematical calculation. What is always of primary importance is the need for a 'faith', for the worship of some idol which can guarantee 'certainties'. The history of Western culture is a succession of phases of submission to an 'infallible cathedra' and the outbreak of revolts with the aim of 'dismantling' the cathedra. The most audacious iconoclasts in this series of revolts (Pascal, Nietzsche, Heidegger, Wittgenstein) are impressive for the intelligence and boldness of the breaks that they attempted but it is also painfully surprising how they have failed to take cognisance of the Heraclitan saying: 'In so far as we share in common (*an koinōnēsōmen*), we say what is true; but when we express our private thoughts (*an idiasōmen*), we say what is false.' Perhaps it is not by chance that the risk of sharing in common – saying what is true (*koinōnein-alētheuein*) manifested itself historically only as a common enterprise (as a culture), not as a methodological discovery.

8. The Embodiment of Apophaticism in a Culture

Greek apophaticism and the criterion of the communal verification of knowledge do not simply constitute philosophical 'principles' of gnoseology. They are (and have been demonstrated historically to be) real axes of a complete mode of life, that is to say, conditions-limits of a cultural nature.

The canon (or possibility) of saying what is true was sought philosophically by the Greeks in the *logos*-mode of the really existent. This *logos*-mode was sought by the architect in the harmony of the dimensions and relations of the 'members' of a building. It was sought by the sculptor in the making of his work an *agalma* (a statue), capable of evoking the exultation (*agalliasē*) of the vision of the really existent. The same quest makes the mystagogic dramaturgy of tragedy a 'revelatory' participation (an experience of contact with the true). It also guides the way the legislator functions. The *logos*-mode of saying what is true is the measure that is embodied in the convention of money: it seeks to balance relations of exchange, to organise in accordance with logos the management-sharing of need.

However, before all these (demonstrative) and particular manifestations of a quest, the priority of saying what is true functions as a goal-axis for the constitution itself of the collectivity, its transformation into *polis*, into a political communion. The second surprising reality in human history that was born on the shores of the Aegean, together with critical thought, is the Greek *polis* (city-state), political art, science and virtue.

The Greeks called *polis* not a settlement whose population had grown but a mode of coexistence: the primary collective pursuit of a passage from a sharing of need to a sharing of truth. *Polis* is a mode of living together with the aim that the human collectivity should realise relations between existents in accordance with *logos*, in the manner in which such relations are attested in the harmony and order of the universe – so as to imitate the *logos*-mode of the decorum of the cosmos, a rational mode of immortality. The Greeks neither depreciated nor overlooked the universal necessity for a community of need; they simply subordinated it to the priority that life should be true, that it should reproduce the eternal rationality of immortal universal beauty, not that some 'overarching' relations should be constructed as a 'superstructure' (*Überbau*) on the 'basis' of material relations (relations of production and exchange), but that the material relations themselves of coexistence (and not only those) should be in accordance with truth (with rational harmony).

The consequences of this quest define, in a very specific way, what the Greeks called political life.

The *polis* was constituted as a common enterprise: all the members of the collective cohabitation participated in the same aspiration. A *polis* cannot be constituted simply by one group, one part of those who live together, while the rest remain without a share in the enterprise.

There are conditions-limits for the formation of a *polis*, that is, principles of political life. This is not to do with 'regulative ordinances', with a code of obligations and rights, but with principles of the art and science of politics, analogous to those which every craft of 'poetic' creation presupposes. Anyone who rejects the rules of the common political endeavour is not subjected to punishments and tortures, but is driven out, is exiled from the *polis*.

Because the aim of the political enterprise is the realisation and manifestation of the mode of existence in accordance with truth, participation in the enterprise is regarded as an honour for the participant. The goal is great and the honour is great, the prerogative of the citizen (*politēs*) being a privilege of responsibility. For that reason, all the citizens without exception participate on equal terms in the power (*kratos*) of exercising responsibility for what is held in common. *Polis* means power-of-the-demos, the totality of citizens. For the Greeks who gave birth to it, the *polis* was inconceivable without democracy.

Every Greek *polis* was a state (*kratos*) formed of the citizens (*polites*) who constituted it, their common enterprise in the service of truth. It was not possible for the enterprise (and the state) to be expanded beyond the limits of the *ekklēsia tou dēmou* (the convocation of the *dēmos*): the assembly that realised and manifested the *polis*. The Greeks refused to expand the state (*kratos*) on the basis of criteria of tribal, ethnic or linguistic homogeneity, to include within the administrators of the state those who had no share in the *political* enterprise (metics and slaves).

Because the prerogative of being a *politēs* was an honor, participation in the common endeavour for truth that constituted the *polis*, the *polites* were chosen by lot – they were not elected by the casting of votes – to the offices of administering each specific responsibility of the needs of the *dēmos*. From the moment someone became a member of the *polis*, he was also self-evidently worthy of any office. The assumption of office by lot and not by election operated, for the first and last time in history, in the ancient Greek *polis*.

For the same reason (because it was a supreme honour to be a *politēs*, a member of a *polis*, to participate in the common endeavour to realise the *logos*-mode of truth), it was also inconceivable in the Greek *poleis* for any citizen to be subjected to any corporal punishment, sanction, penalty or torture. All the contemporary neighbours of the ancient Greeks punished transgressors with whippings, floggings and mutilation. For the Greeks the body of the citizen was sacred; it could not be touched or violated because it was through the body that the achievement of participation in life that was in accordance with truth was actualised and manifested. Socrates was condemned to death by the assembly of the *dēmos*, because even in a democracy the nature of human beings is (and always will be) the same – imperfect and governed by passion. However, there was no executioner to carry out the punishment. Socrates was free to flee the city or, in voluntary obedience to the laws-conditions of the political enterprise, himself to take the cup of hemlock and to drink it.

9. The Counterfeiting of the Ancient Greek Enterprise

Neither of the surprising realities with which the Greeks marked human history, the genesis of critical thought and the genesis of the *polis*-political life, remained permanent achievements of the Greeks. Democracy was not attained for a long period, nor was it attained by every Greek city. As for the fifty-year marvel of Periclean Athens, it died in the horror of the Peloponnesian War. What endured and set its mark on human history were the aims of the Greeks: the aim of the critical verification of knowledge and the aim of political (in accordance with truth) coexistence – measures and criteria for the evaluation, from that time and for always, of every human quest in the field of science or of organised collectivity.

For as long as the goals were conscious aims, the enterprise of truth continued historically, even if under unfavourable and difficult conditions. The Greeks produced their own cultural proposition, a proposition of the primacy of truth and not of the usefulness of sharing (*koinōnein*), not of living for oneself (*idiazein*), even in the centuries when they were subject to the Romans, the Franks and the Turks. The great problem, with critical consequences for the whole of human history, began when the achievements of Greek culture were appropriated, in a manner detached from their aims, by peoples given to a barbarian utilitarianism rooted in the primitiveness of demands centred on the individual. And they appropriated them with the boast that they were continuing the ancient Greek heritage, whereas they were producing a 'culture' in which the Greek presuppositions were inverted.

* * *

The inversion of the cultural presuppositions of the Greeks signifies that instead of the primacy of sharing in truth what was relied on was the primacy of sharing in need. Instead of identifying being true with sharing in accordance with *logos*, truth was identified with individually held certainties. Critical thought and the rational method were distorted to become utilitarian instruments for buttressing self-interest and utilitarianism centred on the individual, the efficacy of power.

It is then that the communal fact (the dynamic becoming of relations of communion) is alienated and turned into a *societas*, 'an association for a common interest'. Interest composes-institutes-activates the collectivity, and individual interests are balanced by commonly accepted contracts (*le contrat social*) that regulate rights and obligations that apply without distinction to all individuals. Contractual living together (with a commonly agreed utilitarian deontology) presupposes, by definition, regulative principles of general application, that is to say, the obligatory bypassing of the uniqueness-dissimilarity-otherness of human existence and the acceptance of individuality as a numerical unit (difference is determined by the number on an identity card, a passport, a tax return, or an insurance document).

When communion is alienated to become a collective (a *societas*, or literally a *société anonyme*), democracy is then, also literally, abused, both as a concept and a reality, and the conditions that defined it for the Greeks are turned on their head. The power (*kratos*) to administer what is held in common is no longer a common enterprise (of all, of the *demos*) so that life may be true; it acquires a utilitarian character, because even truth has been transformed into individual 'convictions' (into an ideology which is chosen by the individual on utilitarian criteria). However, when power is understood as a utilitarian function that is predetermined ideologically (in a utilitarian manner), it can obviously be entrusted to able (shown to be such or by professional qualification) administrators. Thus, the privilege of one who was formerly a *politēs*, or 'citizen', is reduced to the contractual right of every impersonal individual to be 'represented' in the administration of the common life (and of his own life) by others whom the same individual elects at regular intervals.

This retreat (the transformation of the aim) from the sharing of truth to the sharing of need also brings with it the alienation of democracy, turning it into a representative system: from an enterprise of participation in the sharing of responsibility for power, democracy becomes the individual right to elect those who hold power. In comparison with arbitrary imposed tyranny, or royal power transmitted by heredity, the representative system is certainly for the individual a superior mode of the functioning of the collectivity. However, it is a pre-political mode, prior to that which the Greeks called political life, that is, democracy.[21] It is not at all by chance that in the Latin West democracy was called *res publica* ('the public thing'), and in the context of late Modernism we call the 'representative system' 'democracy' – by the same linguistic (historical) arbitrariness that we call today any pornographic product (visual, audial or textual) 'erotic' (érotique, *erotico, erotisch*).

Cut off from the Greek aims of politics, the 'representative democracy' of late Modernity turns out to be very little, if at all, different from the autarkic or tyrannical modes (systems) of the exercise of power. The representation of the *politēs* has been made autonomous; it functions in the absence of the *politēs* and his needs. Power appears to be a balancing of quantitative entities and of counter-opposed 'mechanistic' forces with its own ends, whereas it often serves the private interests of oligarchs. Oligarchic private interest has its institutional expression in political parties: corporations for the claiming and distribution of power. The first, if not the exclusive, aspiration of the parties is to win the vote of the citizen, to seduce him or her by well developed methods of 'brainwashing' and by electoral laws that skilfully falsify the popular will. Forceful advertising (depending on the funds at the disposal of party-political propaganda) seeks to annul the rational and critical capacity of the voter, the function of qualitative evaluation. That is why 'representative democracy' often ends up being synonymous with 'anaxiocracy' (rule by the unworthy), the exaltation of mediocrity, the persecution of quality.

10. Gnoseology Differentiates Cultures

The example of the organisation of the collective life ('politics', as we say improperly today) presents us with a characteristic case of the consequences which result in practice in the way human beings live together from their common position with regard to the need for the verification of knowledge, the commonly accepted criterion of verification – that which in philosophy we call gnoseology. Historically, we can establish that culture (the otherness of a common mode of life) is produced by a common (consolidated in popular practice) gnoseology, not by a common ontology. It is not the content we attribute to truth, but the mode of attestation of cognitive validity that assigns a specific difference to the shaping of the common life (its cultural identity) and assures a historical continuity of cultural particularity. What it is we consider true (how we define the mode of existence of the really

---

21. See *Hē apanthrōpia tou dikaiōmatos*, 3a.

existent) can change without the culture being transformed. However, if the criterion of verification of knowledge changes, the when and how we regard knowledge as being true, then the common mode of life is entirely transformed. Different gnoseologies differentiate cultures, but not different ontologies.

This statement is verified historically by the case of the Greeks. When the Greeks were Christianised (during the first three centuries of Christianity), they adopted an ontology radically different from the attempts at the interpretation of the existent (its endowment with meaning) which had been undertaken (for the first time in history) by Greek philosophers up to that time. However, the proclamation of the Christian Church (the new ontological proposition), addressed in the first place chiefly to the Greek or Hellenised world of the Roman *ecumene*, followed the Greek understanding of how to approach knowledge and verify knowledge, the presuppositions of Greek language and logic, of Greek gnoseology.

The criterion of truth for the Greeks was the experiential-communal participation in knowledge, a criterion which relativises the formulation of knowledge and accords high value to the apophaticism of the formulation: the difference between the knowledge of the signifiers and the comprehension of what is signified. With this same criterion of truth, the empiricism of participation, Christianity brought the Greeks a cognitive content of the word truth entirely different from that which the latter had attributed to it. The mode of access, however, both to the old and to the new thing that was signified was the same: the mode of the Greeks, the mode of participation in relations of shared experience. Christianity proclaimed not a new opinion but a new *ekklēsia*.

The Greeks' *ekklēsia tou dēmou* (assembly of the *dēmos*) sought to realise and manifest the mode of existence and coexistence in accordance with truth, to which the Greeks attested experientially in the relations of rational harmony and in the beauty of the decorum of the universe, a mode that was immutable and immortal. Christianity as an *ekklēsia tōn adelphōn* (an assembly of brothers and sisters) (a fraternity freely achieved and not given by nature) also aimed at the realisation and manifestation of the mode of existence and coexistence which is in accordance with truth, to which the Christians attested experientially in relations of love, in the freedom of love as the causal principle of the existent. The empiricism of knowledge in the case of a Christianised Hellenism clearly appears more coherent and more demanding: from the rational vision and rational harmony of individual acts of contemplation, the Christian Greek passes to a historical grappling with the mode of existence that is in accordance with truth: the historical Jesus, risen from the dead, manifests the possibility that the created can exist in the mode of the uncreated, a mode of freedom from any predetermination of a given substance or nature.

Thus, the Trinitarian God of the Christian Church is, as a rational proposition, the Greek's freedom, his exit from imprisonment in the impasse of necessity: necessity which as an *a priori* given rationality (*xynos logos*: common *logos*) precedes and predetermines the existential fact, and excludes creation from nothing, the emerging otherness of rational existence, and the unforeseeable – in sum, all of history. The *logos* of the existent precedes its existence in ancient Greek ontology and determines its being – even God, as prime mover, or however else we conceive him, is obliged, by the *logos* of his existence, to be that which he is, to exist as he exists. The principle (the original point of departure) of existence and of every existent (a principle that precedes even God) is the necessity of rational predetermination – Greek thought is incapable of conceiving of the possibility of existential freedom, of the original indeterminacy of the existential event.

By contrast, Christian (ecclesial-shared) experience proclaims a God who is the causal principle of existence and of existents, free from any necessary predetermination of his existence, free from any (inexplicably) given essence. A God who wills to exist and whose free will 'hypostasises' the mode of his existence as the freedom of love – with the semantic 'relativity' of our language we say: he is the Father. The word indicates not the name of an individual (Zeus, Ahura Mazda) but the cause of the creative (*demiourgikē*) operation that inaugurates the existential event, he who, outside time in a loving manner, freely hypostasises his existence and constitutes it as a loving communion of hypostases: the Father 'generates' the Son and causes the Spirit 'to proceed'. By these three words, Father, Son, Spirit, that indicate referentiality and relation (not the ontic autonomy of individuality) and, similarly, by the definitions ingenerate, generate, that proceeds, the apophatic language of ecclesial experience succeeds in being able to say that God is love. For the causal principle of existence and of existents is a personal (self-conscious, rational) freedom, not an impersonal (mechanical, causally inexplicable) impersonal necessity.

Bibliography

Works by Christos Yannaras

In almost all his books of the last decade Yannaras has appended a list of his published works.[1] This is a kind of official bibliography which understandably does not record the author's innumerable articles written in various languages (only partly included in the published collections) but it does at least record all his books published in Greek. I shall rely fundamentally on this official bibliography, making nevertheless some modifications.

I shall therefore list the books by dividing them into five sections, the first four corresponding to the classifications adopted by the author himself in *Ta kath' eauton* and repeated successively in various ways, with the fifth section added by me in order to bring together the liturgical texts that Yannaras has personally produced (and published anonymously) with the aim of allowing the ontological significance of liturgical celebrations to emerge more clearly.

---

1. [Yannaras also lists all the translations of his books. In Western European languages English and Italian translations lead the field and are given in full below. French versions have also been published of the following six works: *De l'absence et de l'inconnaissance de Dieu* (*Heidegger kai Areopagitēs ē peri apousias kai agnōsias tou Theou*) in 1971; *La liberté de la morale* (*Hē eleutheria tou ēthous*) in 1983; *Philosophie sans rupture* (*Schediasma eisagōgēs stē philosophia*) in 1984; *La foi vivante de l'Église* (*Alphabētari tēs pistēs*) in 1989; *Verité et unité de l'Église* (*Alētheia kai henotēta tēs Ekklēsias*) in 1989; and *Variations sur le Cantique des Cantiques* (*Scholio sto Asma tōn Asmatōn*) in 1992. There is only one German translation: *Person und Eros* (*To prosōpo kai ho erōs*) published in 1982. Besides these, a large number of works have been translated into Eastern European languages, particularly Romanian, Serbian and Russian. Trans.]

I first give the Greek title (in transliteration) followed by an English translation, indicating so far as possible the first and most recent edition of each volume. Because the various editions of the same work have sometimes modified the title as well as the content, to a greater or lesser degree, I record, so far as possible, the various editions with the changed title, drawing attention to the fact that up to now Yannaras has often numbered the editions successively without regard to the change of title.

1.1. Ta Philosophika *(Philosophical works)*

Hē theologia tēs apousias kai tēs agnōsias tou Theou, me anaphores stis Areopagitikes syngraphes kai ston Martin Heidegger (The theology of the absence and unknowability of God, with reference to the Areopagitical writings and Martin Heidegger), n.p., Athens, 1967

To ontologikon periechomenon tēs theologikēs ennoias tou prosōpou (The ontological content of the concept of the person) (Athens: Tip. Proodos, 1970)

To prosōpo kai ho erōs: Theologiko dokimio ontologias (Person and eros: A theological essay on ontology) (Athens: Papazēsē, 1976)

Schediasma eisagōgēs stē philosophia (An outline introduction to philosophy), first edition in two volumes (Athens: Domos, 1980-81); second edition and four reprints (Athens: Domos, 1988-2002 [fifth]); seventh edition with additions and the subtitle, *Hē hellēnikē optikē kai hē dytikē antistrophē tēs* (The Greek perspective and its western reversal) (Athens: Ikaros, 2013)

To prosōpo kai ho erōs (Person and eros)[2] (Athens: Domos, 1987 [fourth])

Orthos logos kai koinōnikē praktikē (Correct reason and social practice) (Athens: Domos, 1984, 2006 [fourth])

Protaseis kritikēs ontologias (Propositions of a critical ontology) (Athens: Domos, 1985; Athens: Ikaros, 2010 [fourth, with modifications])

Heidegger kai Areopagitēs: Hē theologia tēs apousias kai tēs agnōsias tou Theou (Heidegger and the Areopagite: The theology of the absence and unknowability of God) (Athens: Domos, 1988 [second], 2006 [fifth])

To pragmatiko kai to phantasiōdes stēn politikē oikonomia (The real and the imaginary in the political economy) (Athens: Domos, 1989, 2006 [third])

Meta-neōterikē meta-physikē (Postmodern metaphysics) (Athens: Domos, 1993, 2005 [second])

Hē apanthrōpia tou dikaiōmatos (The inhumanity of right) (Athens: Domos, 1997, 2006 [third])

To rhēto kai to arrhēto: Ta glōssika oria realismou tēs metaphysikēs (What can be said and what cannot be said: The linguistic limits of the realism of metaphysics) (Athens: Ikaros, 1999, 2008 [second])

Ontologia tēs schesēs (Ontology of relation) (Athens: Ikaros, 2004, 2008 [second])

To ainigma tou kakou (The enigma of evil) (Athens: Ikaros, 2008, 2009 [second])

Exi philosophikes zōgraphies: 'Ekomisa eis tēn technēn' (Six philosophical pictures: 'I have brought to art') (Athens: Ikaros, 2011, 2012 [second])

---

2. On this work and the numbering of the editions, see p. 35, note 5 above.

1.2. Technēmata *(Artefacts)*

Peina kai dipsa: Dōdeka paradoxa dokimia (Hunger and thirst: Twelve paradoxical essays) (Athens: Skapanē, 1961)
Peina kai dipsa: Deuterē ekdosē me prosthēkes (Hunger and thirst: Second edition with additions) (Athens: Grēgorē, 1969, 1997 [fifth])
Hē kokkinē plateia kai ho theios Arthouros (Red Square and Uncle Arthur) (Athens: Domos, 1986, 2006 [fifth])
Kataphygion ideōn: Martyria (Refuge of ideas: Testimony) (Athens: Domos, 1987, 2007 [seventh])
Scholio sto Asma Asmatōn (A comment on the Song of Songs) (Athens: Domos, 1990, 2003 [sixth])
Ta kath' eauton (Personal memories) (Athens: Ikaros, 1995, 2005 [fourth])
Anthologēma technēmatōn (Anthology of artefacts) (Athens: Kastaniōtēs, 1991, 1993 [second])
Aoristē Hellada: Kontserto gia dyo apodēmies (Undefined Greece: A concerto for two emigrations) (Athens: Domos, 1994, 1999 [fourth])
Alphabētari tou neoellēna: Keimena epikairēs hellēnikēs autosynēdēsias (Primer of the modern Greek: Texts of current Greek self-awareness), *Anthologēsē* (A selection) (Athens: Patakē, 2000, 2004 [ninth])

1.3. Ta Theologika *(Theological works)*

Timioi me tēn Orthodoxia: Neoellēnika theologika dokimia (Honest with Orthodoxy: Modern Greek theological essays) (Athens: Astēr, 1968)
Hē eleutheria tou ēthous: Dokimes gia mia orthodoxē theōrēsē tēs ēthikēs (The freedom of morality: Attempts at an Orthodox vision of ethics) (Athens: Athēna, 1970)
Hē metaphysikē tou sōmatos: Spoudē ston Iōannē tēs Klimakos (The metaphysics of the body: A study on John Climacus) (Athens: Dōdōnē, 1971)
Orthodoxia kai Dysē: Hē theologia stēn Hellada sēmera (Orthodoxy and the West: Theology in Greece today) (Athens: Athēna, 1972)
Hē apologētikē sta horia tēs orthodoxou theologias (Apologetics in the context of Orthodox theology) (Athens: Grēgorē, 1975, 1989 [second])
Alētheia kai henotēta tēs Ekklēsias (Truth and unity of the Church) (Athens: Grēgorē, 1977, 1997 [second])
Hē eleutheria tou ēthous (The freedom of morality), second revised edition (Athens: Grēgorē, 1979)
Alphabētari tēs pistēs (A primer of faith) (Athens: Domos, 1983, 2006 [fourteenth])
Erōtikōn amphilogia ē peri libellopragmonos monachou (Controversy on erotic matters or on a libellous monk) (Athens: Domos, 1989)
Orthodoxia kai Dysē stē neōterē Hellada (Orthodoxy and the West in modern Greece) (Athens: Domos, 1992)
Heortologika palinōdoumena (Liturgical feasts revisited) (Athens: Akritas, 1999)
Hē eleutheria tou ēthous (The freedom of morality), third revised edition (Athens: 2002, 2011 [fourth])
Enantia stē thrēskeia (Against religion) (Athens: Ikaros, 2006, 2010 [fourth])
Hē Eurōpē gennēthēke apo to 'Schisma' (Europe was born from the 'Schism') (Athens: Ikaros, 2015)

1.4. Chronographiai *(Newspaper articles)*

Hē krisē tēs prophēteias (The crisis of prophecy), *Synoro*, 1964 (Athens: 'Astēr' & E. Papadēmētriou, 1968)

Hē krisē tēs prophēteias (1963-1966) (The crisis of prophecy [1963-66]) (Athens: Domos, 1981 [third]; Ikaros, 2010 [fourth])

To pronomio tēs apelpisias (1971-1973): Sēmeiōseis gia mia kritikē anametrēsē me to adiexodo tou dytikou ē katanalōtikou politismou kai tēn autosyneidēsia tēs Orthodoxias (The privilege of despair [1971-73]: Notes for a critical approach to the impasse of western or consumerist culture and to the self-awareness of Orthodoxy) (Athens: Grēgorē, 1973)

Kephalaia Politikēs Theologias (1974-1975) (Chapters on political theology [1974-75]) (Athens: Papazēsē, 1976; Grēgorē, 1983 [second])

Hē neoellēnikē tautotēta (1976-1977) (Modern Greek identity [1976-77]) (Athens: Grēgorē, 1978, 2001 [fourth])

Kritikes Parembaseis (Critical interventions) (Athens: Domos, 1983, 1987 [second with additions], 1992 [third])

Finis Greciae (1985-1989): Thrēnētikē eikasia (*Finis Greciae* [1985-89]: A grieving conjecture) (Athens: Kastianiōtē, 1992 [second])

To keno stēn trechousa politikē (The void in current politics) (Athens: Kastaniōtē, 1992 [second])

Helladika proteleutia (1990) (Penultimate signs for Greece [1990]) (Athens: Kastaniōtē, 1992)

Chōra hypocheiria paigniou (1989-1990) (A nation reduced to a plaything [1989-90]) (Athens: Kastaniōtē, 1994)

Politikē chronographia 1991: Aperiskeptōs autocheires (Political chronicle 1991: Thoughtless suicides) (Athens: Kastaniōtē, 1994)

Hellēnotropos politikē: Ex antithetou kritēria kai protaseis (Politics Greek-style: Contradictory criteria and propositions) (Athens: Ikaros, 1996)

Aphellēnismou parepomena: Politikē chronographia 1993 (Consequences of de-Hellenisation: Political articles 1993) (Athens: Indiktos, 1997; Kaktos, 2005 [second])

Antistaseis stēn allotriōsē: Epikairē kritikē schoinobasia (Resistances to alienation: Today's critical tightrope-walking) (Athens: Ikaros, 1987, 2008 [second])

Politismos, to kentriko problēma tēs politikēs: Politikē chronographia 1996 (Culture, the central problem of politics: Political articles 1996) (Athens: Indiktos, 1997; Kaktos, 2005 [second])

Ichnēlasia noēmatos: Politikē, koinōnia, paideia stēn Hellada sēmera: Chronographia 1997 (On the tracks of a meaning: Politics, society, education in Greece today: Newspaper articles 1997) (Athens: Libanē, 1998)

Hē parakmē hōs proklēsē (Decadence as a challenge) (Athens: Libanē, 1999)

Hellēnikē hetoimotēta gia tēn eurōpaikēn henopoiēsē: kritikoi epikairikoi entopismoi (Greek readiness for European unification: current critical positionings) (Athens: Libanē, 2000)

Politistikē diplōmatia: Protheōria hellēnikou schediasmou (Cultural diplomacy: A preliminary review of a Greek project) (Athens: Ikaros, 2001, 2003 [second])

Paideia kai glōssa: Epikairika palinodoumena (Education and language: Current retractions) (Athens: Patakē, 2001 [second])

Bibliography

Hē Aristera hōs Dexia: Hē Dexia hōs pantomima: Stoicheia kritikēs analysēs tou neoellēnikou mēdenismou (The Left as Right: The Right as pantomime: Elements of a critical analysis of modern Greek nihilism) (Athens: Patakē, 2001 [second])
Kommatokratia: Otan hoi polites hyperpsēphizoun tē leēlasia tēs zōēs tous (Partyocracy: When citizens vote in favour of the plundering of their life) (Athens: Patakē, 2002, 2004 [third])
'Eis mikron gennaioi': Hodēgies chrēseōs ('Generous in small things': Instructions for use) (Athens: Patakē, 2003)
Prophorikē amesotēta (Verbal immediacy) (Thessaloniki: Ianos, 2003)
Hē logikē archizei me ton erōta: Kritikē chronographia (Logic begins with eros: Critical articles) (Athens: Ikaros, 2004)
Koinōniokentrikē Politikē: Kritēria: Epikairikes dokimes (Communocentric politics: Criteria: Current attempts) (Athens: Hestia, 2005)
Machomenē anelpistia (A combative hopelessness) (Athens: Hestia, 2007 [second])
Epainos psēphou timorētikēs: Hē politikē epikairotēta hōs hyparxiakē proklēsē kai dokimasia graphēs (Praise of a punitive vote: The current political situation as an existential challenge and proof of Scripture) (Athens: Ianos, 2007, 2008 [second])
Hē katarrheusē tou politikou systēmatos stēn Hellada sēmera (The collapse of the political system in Greece today) (Athens: Ianos, 2008 [second])
To politiko zētoumeno stēn Hellada sēmera (In search of a policy in Greece today) (Athens: Ianos, 2010 [second])
Kata kephalēn kalliergeia (hē antistasē stēn parakmē): Epiphyllides 2009 (Culture *per capita*: Resistance in decline: Newspaper columns 2009) (Athens: Ianos, 2010, 2011 [second])
Hē politikē gonimotēta tēs orgēs: Epiphyllides 2010 (The political fecundity of anger: Newspaper columns 2010) (Athens: Ianos, 2011)
Hē katastrophē hōs eukairia: Epiphyllides 2011 (Catastrophe as opportunity: Newspaper columns 2011) (Athens: Ianos, 2012, 2013 [third])
To problēma mas einai politiko, ochi oikonomiko: Epiphyllides 2012 (Our problem is political, not economic: Newspaper columns 2012) (Athens: Ianos, 2013)
Hē hellēnikotēta hōs poiotēta kai hōs ntropē: Epiphyllides 2013 (Greekness as a quality and as a cause for shame: Newspaper columns 2013) (Athens: Ianos 2014)
Finis Greciae: Epiphyllides 1985-1990 (*Finis Greciae*: Newspaper columns 1985-90) (Athens: Ianos, 2014)
Topos tou anoikeiou tropou: Hē Hellada tou 2014: Epiphyllides (Place of an inconvenient mode: Greece in 2014: Newspaper columns) (Athens: Ianos, 2015)
Tēn alētheia katamata: Epiphyllides 2015 (Looking truth in the eye: Newspaper columns 2015) (Athens: Ianos, 2016)

1.5. Leitourgika *(Liturgical texts)*

Nea ekklēsiastikē Akolouthia tou Mystēriou tou Gamou syntetheisa kai proteinomenē tēi Ekklēsiai hypo anōnymou tinos engamou (A new ecclesiastical rite of the sacrament of matrimony composed and offered to the Church by an anonymous married person) (Athens: Domos, Christmas 1997)

Nea ekklēsiastikē Akolouthia eis kekoimēmenous syntetheisa kai proteinomenē tēi Ekklēsiai hypo anōnymou tinos tōn perileipomenōn (A new ecclesiastical funeral service composed and offered to the Church by an anonymous person among those left behind) (Athens: Domos, 2008)

Nea ekklēsiastikē Akolouthia tou Mystēriou tou Baptismatos syntetheisa kai proteinomenē tēi Ekklēsiai hypo anōnymou tinos tōn bebaptismenōn (A new ecclesiastical rite of the sacrament of baptism composed and offered to the Church by an anonymous baptized person) (Athens: Domos, 2012)

Hē ekklēsiastikē Eucharistia hōs aitoumeno epikairikēs metagraphēs, hypo anōnymou tinos tōn aitoumenōn (The ecclesiastical Eucharist in so far as it calls for a transcription into the current language, by an anonymous person who requests it) (Athens: Domos, 2012)

2. Italian translations of Yannaras' writings

'La morale della libertà: Presupposti per una visione ortodossa della morale', in Ch. Yannaras, R. Mehle and J.M. Aubert, *La legge della libertà: evangelo e morale*, translated from the French (Paris, 1972) by Franco Follo (Milan: Jaca Book, 1973) pp. 15-66

Ignoranza e conoscenza di Dio, translated by Piero Scazzoso from the original Greek text of Christos Yannaras (Athens, 1971) (Milan: Jaca Book, 1973)

'Il matrimonio, sacramento di manifestazione della verità della persona nella tradizione ortodossa', *Communio* 3, no. 4 (1974) pp. 50-55

La libertà dell'ethos: Alle radici della crisi morale in occidente, translated by Basilio Petrà from the second revised edition of *Hē eleutheria tou ēthous* (Athens: Grēgorē, 1979) (Bologna: EDB, 1984)

'Influssi filofofici sulla mistica della patristica greca', in Jean-Marie van Cagne (ed), *La mistica*, translated from the French (Bologna: EDB, 1992) pp. 75-81

La fede dell'esperienza ecclesiale: Introduzione alla teologia ortodossa, translated from the French version of *Alphabētari tēs pistēs* (*La foi vivante de l'Église: Introduction à la théologie orthodoxe*) by Pietro Crespi and revised on the basis of the Greek text by Basilio Petrà (Brescia: Queriniana, 1993)

La buona notizia sull'uomo (Magnano: Qiqajon [Community of Bose], 1995)

Variazioni sul Cantico dei Cantici, Italian translation from the Greek text of *Scholio sto Asma Asmatōn* by Antonio Ranzolin and revised by Vassilis Kalogerakis and Kallinikos Lasaridis (Milan-Schio: CENS-Interlogos, Cernusco sul Naviglio, 1992; new edition Magnano: Qiqajon [Community of Bose], 2012)

Heidegger e Dionigi Areopagita, assenza e ignoranza di Dio, Italian translation by Antonio Fyrigos of *Heidegger kai Areopagitēs: Hē theologia tēs apousias kai tēs agnōsias tou Theou* (Athens: Domos, 1987 [second]) (Rome: Città Nuova, 1995)

Verità e unità della Chiesa, Italian translation by Antonio Edi Bressan, Vassilis Kalogerakis, Antonio Ranzolin and Ester Reghellin of *Alētheia kai henotēta tēs Ekklēsias* (Athens: Grēgorē, 1977) (Sotto il Monte (BG)-Schio (VI): Servitium editrice-Interlogos, 1995)

'L'icona nella riflessione filosofica', in A. Hart, A. Jevtic, J.-C. Larchet, St Skliris and Ch. Yannaras, *In un'altra forma: Percorsi di iniziazione all'icona* (Sotto il Monte

(BG)-Schio (VI): Servitium editrice-Interlogos, 1996) pp. 61-100; a translation from the Greek by Antonio Ranzolin and Vassilis Kalogerakis of Chapter 2 of Part III of *To prosōpo kai ho erōs* (Athens: Domos, 1987 [fourth])

'*Matrimonio e monachesimo: le vie dell'eros*', in S.S. Fotiou, A. Marini, Gh. Patronos and Ch. Yannaras, *La cella del vino: Parole sull'amore e sul matrimonio* (Sotto il Monte (BG)-Schio (VI): Servitium editrice-Interlogos, 1997 pp. 175-85; a translation from the Greek by Antonio Ranzolin, revised by Vassilis Kalogerakis, of an article first published in *Synoro* 34 (1965) pp. 111-17 and, subsequently, in the volume *Hē krisē tēs prophēteias* (Athens: Domos, 1988 [second]) pp. 87-99

'*L'"antifemminismo" della Chiesa*', in St S. Fotiou, A. Marini, Gh. Patronos and Ch. Yannaras, *La cella del vino: Parole sull'amore e sul matrimonio*, pp. 187-92; a translation from the Greek by Antonio Ranzolin, revised by Vassilis Kalogerakis, of a short piece which appeared in a collection of essays, *Erōs kai gamos* (Athens, 1972) pp. 163-71

(No title) in S.S. Fotiou, A. Marini, Gh. Patronos and Ch. Yannaras, *La cella del vino: Parole sull'amore e sul matrimonio*, pp. 193-204; a translation from the Greek by Antonio Ranzolin, revised by Vassilis Kalogerakis, of the second part of *Erōtikōn amphilogia ē peri libellopragmonos monachou* (Athens: Domos, 1989)

'*Il ruolo della diaspora russa nella formazione della coscienza teologica contemporanea*', in Adalberto Mainardi (ed), *La notte della chiesa russa: Atti del VII Convegno ecumenico internazionale di spiritualità russa 'La Chiesa ortodossa russa dal 1943 ai nostri giorni'*, Bose, 15-18 September 1999, translated from the French by Laura Marino (Magnano: Qiqajon [Community of Bose], 2000) pp. 243-49

'*Amore umano e amore Cristiano*', in Ch. Yannaras and G. Khodr, *Amore umano e amore cristiano* (Magnano: Monastery of Bose, 2001)

Ontologia della relazione, Italian translation of *Ontologia tēs scheseēs* (Athens: Ikaros, 2004), edited with an introductory essay by Basilio Petrà (Troina: Città Aperta, 2010)

Contro la religione, Italian translation by Basilio Petrà of *Enantia stē thrēskeia* (Athens: Ikaros, 2006) (Magnano: Qiqajon [Community of Bose], 2011)

'*L'ethos dell'arte liturgica*', in various authors, *Ars liturgica: l'arte a servizio della liturgia* (Magnano: Qiqajon [Community of Bose], 2012) pp. 203-34

'*Il realismo ontologico di ciò che si spera dopo la morte: Conclusioni da alcuni riferimenti concisi di Massimo il Confessore*', in *La sapienza del cuore: Omaggio a Enzo Bianchi* (Turin: Einaudi, 2013) pp. 377-84

La libertà dell'ethos, the Italian translation of 1984 corrected and revised by Basilio Petrà on the basis of the third Greek edition of 2002, with a preface by Basilio Petrà (Magnano: Qiqajon [Community of Bose], 2014

3. *English translations of Yannaras' writings*

'Orthodoxy and the West', translated by Theodore Stylianopoulos, *Eastern Churches Review* 3, no. 3 (1971), pp. 286-300; reprinted in A.J. Philippou (ed), *Orthodoxy, Life and Freedom: Essays in Honour of Archbishop Iakovos* (Oxford: Studion Publications, 1973) pp. 130-47

'Theology in Present-Day Greece', translated from the original French by Angeline Bouchard, *St Vladimir's Theological Quarterly* 16 (1972), pp. 195-214

The Meaning of Reality: Essays on Existence and Communion, Eros and History, edited by Fr Gregory Edwards and Herman A. Middleton (Los Angeles: Sebastian Press and Indiktos, 2011)

'A Note on Political Theology', translated by Steven Peter Tsichlis, *St Vladimir's Seminary Quarterly* 27, no. 1 (1983), pp. 53-56; reprinted in *The Meaning of Reality*, pp. 149-52

The Freedom of Morality, a translation of *Hē eleutheria tou ēthous* (Athens: Grēgorē, 1979) by Elizabeth Briere (Crestwood, NY: St Vladimir's Seminary Press, 1984)

Elements of Faith: An Introduction to Orthodox Theology, a translation of *Alphabētari tēs pistēs* (Athens: Domos, 1983) by Keith Schram (Edinburgh: T. & T. Clark, 1991)

'The Church in the Postcommunist World', *International Journal for the Study of the Christian Church* 3, no. 1 (2003), pp. 29-46; a different version, under the title 'The Church in Post-Communist Europe', was published as a separate booklet in the same year by Interorthodox Press of Berkeley, California, and reprinted in *The Meaning of Reality*, pp.123-43

Postmodern Metaphysics, a translation of *Meta-neōterikē meta-physikē* (Athens: Domos, 1993) by Norman Russell (Brookline, MA: Holy Cross Orthodox Press, 2004)

'Human Rights and the Orthodox Church', in E. Clapsis (ed), *The Orthodox Churches in a Pluralistic World: An Ecumenical Conversation* (Brookline, MA: Holy Cross Orthodox Press, 2004) pp. 83-89; reprinted in *The Meaning of Reality*, pp. 45-50

On the Absence and Unknowability of God: Heidegger and the Areopagite, with an Introduction by Andrew Louth, a translation of *Heidegger kai Areopagitēs: Hē theologia tēs apousias kai tēs agnōsias tou Theou* (Athens: Domos, 1988), translated by Haralambos Ventis (London: T. & T. Clark International, 2005)

Variations on the Song of Songs, a translation of *Scholio sto Asma Asmatōn* (Athens: Domos, 1990) by Norman Russell (Brookline, MA: Holy Cross Orthodox Press, 2005)

Orthodoxy and the West: Hellenic Self-identity in the Modern Age, a translation of *Orthodoxia kai Dysē stē neōterē Hellada* (Athens: Domos, 1992) by Peter Chamberas and Norman Russell (Brookline, MA: Holy Cross Orthodox Press, 2006)

Person and Eros, a translation of *To prosōpo kai ho erōs* (Athens: Domos, 1987) by Norman Russell (Brookline, MA: Holy Cross Orthodox Press, 2007)

'A revised Orthodox ceremony of marriage?' a translation of *Nea ekklēsiastikē Akolouthia tou Mystēriou tou Gamou syntetheisa kai proteinomenē tēi Ekklēsiai hypo anōnymou tinos engamou* (Athens: Domos, 1997) by Andrew Louth, *Sobornost* 29, no. 2 (2007), pp. 51-74; reprinted in *The Meaning of Reality*, pp. 93-113

Relational Ontology, a translation of *Ontologia tēs scheseōs* (Athens: Ikaros, 2004) by Norman Russell (Brookline, MA: Holy Cross Orthodox Press, 2011)

The Enigma of Evil, a translation of *To ainigma tou kakou* (Athens: Ikaros, 2008) by Norman Russell (Brookline, MA: Holy Cross Orthodox Press, 2012)

Against Religion: The Alienation of the Ecclesial Event, a translation of *Enantia stē thrēskeia* (Athens: Ikaros, 2006) by Norman Russell (Brookline, MA: Holy Cross Orthodox Press, 2013)

'A New Funeral Service for the Orthodox?' a translation of *Nea ekklēsiastikē Akolouthia eis kekoimēmenous syntetheisa kai proteinomenē tēi Ekklēsiai hypo anōnymou tinos tōn perileipomenōn* (Athens: Domos, 2008) by Andrew Louth, *Sobornost* 35, nos 1-2 (2013), pp. 123-35

4. Bibliography on Yannaras

Angelēs, A., et al., *Chrēstos Giannaras* (Athens: Manifesto, 2015)

Bonner, G., 'Christianity and the Modern World-View', *Eastern Churches Review* 5, no. 1 (1973), pp. 1-15

Depraz, N., 'Das Individuum als Beziehungswesen: Die Marxinterpretation Michel Henrys im Vergleich mit F.J. Varela und Ch. Yannaras', in Emil Angehrn and Julia Scheidegger (eds), *Metaphysik des Individuums: Die Marx-Interpretation Michel Henrys und ihre Aktualität* (Freiburg im Breisgau: Karl Haber, 2011) pp. 127–49

Ghio, G., '*La deliberazione vitale come origine ultima della certezza applicate a Dio: Indagine sugli elementi d'ignoranza presenti nella certezza*', Tesi Gregoriana, Serie teologia 108 (Rome: Pontificia Università Gregoriana, 2004)

Gnau, D., 'Person werden: Theologische Anthropologie im Werk der gegen wärtigen orthodoxen Theologen Panagiotis Nellas, Christos Yannaras und Ioannis Zizioulas',Inauguraldissertation zur Erlangung der Doktorwürde der Theologischen Fakultät der Albert-Ludwigs-Universität, Freiburg im Breisgau, April 2005

———, *Person werden: Zu Wesen und Bestimmung des Menschen in der Theologie von Panagiotis Nellas, Christos Yannaras und Ioannis Zizioulas* (Würzburg: Echter, 2015)

Grigoropoulou, E., 'The Early Development of the Thought of Christos Yannaras', thesis submitted for the Degree of Doctor of Philosophy, Department of Theology and Religion, University of Durham, 7 October 2008

Jensen, A.S., 'Schleiermacher and Bonhoeffer as Negative Theologians: A Western Response to Some Eastern Challenges', *St Mark's Review* 215, no. 1 (2011), pp. 7-20

Kalaitzidis, P., '*Hellēnikotēta kai Antidytikismos stē "Theologia tou '60"*' (Greekness and anti-westernism in the 'Theology of the 1960s'), doctoral dissertation, Department of Theology, Aristotelian University of Thessaloniki, 2008, especially pp. 209-584

———, '*Hē anakalypsē tēs hellēnikotētas kai ho theologikos antidykismos*' (The discovery of Greekness and theological anti-westernism), in P. Kalaitzidis, Th.N. Papathanasiou and Th. Ampatzidis (eds), *Anataraxeis stē metapolemikē theologia: Hē 'theologia tou '60'*, pp. 429-514

Kalaitzidis, P., Th. N. Papathanasiou and Th. Ampatzidis (eds), *Anataraxeis stē metapolemikē theologia: Hē 'theologia tou '60'* (Turmoil in post-war theology: The 'theology of the 1960s') (Athens: Indiktos, 2009); all the contributors touch in some way on Christos Yannaras' mode of thought and cultural role

Larchet, J.-C., *Personne et nature: La Trinité – Le Christ – L'homme: Contributions aux dialogues interorthodoxe et interchrétien contemporains* (Paris: Cerf, 2011) pp. 207-396

Loudovikos, N., 'Ho erōs hōs hodos theologias kai eleutherias: Hē erōtikē amphilogia tou Chrēstou Giannara' (Eros as a way of theology and of freedom: The erotic ambiguity of Christos Yannaras), in idem, *Hoi tromoi tou prosōpou kai ta basana tou erōta: Kritikoi stochasmoi gia mia metaneōterikē theologikē ontologia* (The terrors of the person and the torments of eros: Critical thoughts toward a postmodern theological ontology) (Athens and Thessaloniki: Harmos, 2009) pp. 67-111; this essay reproduces, with corrections and additions, the author's contribution to *Anataraxeis stē metapolemikē theologia: Hē 'theologia tou '60'*, pp. 293-314, under the title '*Ho erōs hōs hodos theologias kai eleutherias, me kyria anaphora sto ergo tou Chrēstou Giannara*' (Eros as a way of theology and freedom, with particular reference to the work of Christos Yannaras)

Louth, A., 'Some Recent Works by Christos Yannaras in English Translation', *Modern Theology* 25, no. 2 (2009), pp. 329-40

———, 'Lay Theologians: 2 Dimitris Koutroubis, Christos Yannaras, Stelios Ramfos', in idem, *Modern Orthodox Thinkers: From the* Philokalia *to the present* (London: SPCK, 2015) pp. 247-63

Millsaps, K.T., 'The Development of Apophatic Theology from the Pre-Socratics to the Early Christian Fathers', East Tennessee State University, Electronic Theses and Dissertations (Paper 2178), 2006

Mitralexis, S., 'Person, Eros, Critical Ontology: An Attempt to Recapitulate Christos Yannaras' Philosophy', *Sobornost* 34, no. 1 (2012), pp. 33-40

———, 'Ever-moving Repose: The Notion of Time in Maximus the Confessor's Philosophy through the Perspective of a Relational Ontology', doctoral thesis in Philosophy, Department of Philosophy, Freie Universität Berlin, 2014

———, 'Relational Ontologies in Dialogue: Christos Yannaras' and Joseph Kaipayil's Distinct "Relational Ontologies"', *Philosophia*, 21 August 2014: http://philosophy-e.com/sotiris-mitralexis-relational-ontologies-in-dialogue-christos-yannaras-and-joseph-kaipayils-distinct-relational-ontologies/

Mpenzos, M.P., *To mellon tou parelthontos: Kritikē eiagōgē stē theologia tēs orthodoxias* (The future of the past: A critical introduction to the theology of Orthodoxy) (Athens: Harmos, 1993)

Murray, R., 'A Brief Comment on Dr Yannaras' Article', *Eastern Churches Review* 3, no. 3 (1971), pp. 306-7

Nichols, A., 'Christos Yannaras and Theological Ethics', in idem, *Light from the East: Authors and Themes in Orthodox Theology* (London: Sheed & Ward, 1995) pp. 181-93

Nissiotis, N., 'Orthodoxy and the West: A Response', *The Greek Orthodox Theological Review* 17 (1972), pp. 131-42

Panagiatopoulos, A.St., 'Physē kai prosōpo kata ton Chrēsto Giannara' (Nature and person according to Christos Yannaras), postgraduate dissertation under the direction of Prof. G. Martzelos, Department of Theology, School of Theology, Aristotle University of Thessaloniki, December 2011

Papanikolaou, A., 'Orthodoxy, Post-Modernism, and Ecumenism: The Difference that Divine-Human Communion Makes', *Journal of Ecumenical Studies* 42, no. 4 (Fall 2007), pp. 527-46
———, 'Personhood and its Exponents in Twentieth-Century Orthodox Theology', in Mary B. Cunningham and Elizabeth Theokritoff (eds), *The Cambridge Companion to Orthodox Christian Theology* (Cambridge: Cambridge University Press, 2008) pp. 232-45
———, 'Orthodox Theology in the Twentieth Century', in Staale Johannes Kristiansen and Svein Rise (eds), *Key Theological Thinkers: From Modern to Postmodern* (Burlington, VT, and Farnham: Ashgate, 2013) pp. 53-62
———, *The Mystical as Political: Democracy and Non-Radical Orthodoxy* (Notre Dame, IN: University of Notre Dame Press, 2012)
Payne, D.P., 'An Eastern Orthodox Critique of Rawlsian Liberalism: The Personal Ontology of Christos Yannaras', at http://sbulgakov.livejournal.com/43546.html, posted on 27 July 2006
———, 'Orthodoxy, Islam and the "Problem" of the West: A Comparison of the Liberation Theologies of Christos Yannaras and Sayyid Qutb', *Religion, State and Society* 36, no. 4 (2008), pp. 435-50
———, *The Revival of Political Hesychasm in Contemporary Orthodox Thought: The Political Hesychasm of John S. Romanides and Christos Yannaras* (Lanham, MD: Lexington Books, 2011)
———, 'The "Relational Ontology" of Christos Yannaras: The Hesychastic Influence on the Understanding of the Person in the Thought of Christos Yannaras', at https://www.academia.edu/1479462
Petrà, B., *'Figure spirituali greche* (1): Apostolos Makrakis (1831-1905)', *Unitas* (Roma) 30 (1975), pp. 4-26
———, *'Figure spirituali greche* (2): Eusebio Matthopoulos (1849-1929) e la fraternità di Zoi', *Unitas* (Roma) 30 (1975), pp. 91-119
———, 'Osservazioni su un recente volume di Christos Yannaras', *Unitas* (Roma) 32 (1978), pp. 18-26
———, 'Christos Yannaras e la verità dell'ethos', *Rivista di teologia morale* 16, no. 64 (1984), pp. 539-48
———, 'Cristo Salvatore della verità personale dell'uomo nella riflessione ortodossa contemporanea', in *La coscienza morale oggi: Omaggio al prof. Domenico Capone* (Rome: Editiones Academiae Alphonsianae, 1987) pp. 373-405
———, *Tra cielo e terra: Introduzione alla teologia ortodossa contemporanea* (Bologna: EDB, 1992) pp. 95-100, 187-92
———, 'Dal pensiero della differenza al pensiero dell'unità: Nota su un'opera di Christos Yannaras', *Vivens homo* 6 (1995), pp. 163-80
———, '"Communio" ecclesiale e genesi del soggetto morale', in L. Melina and P. Zanor (eds), *Quale dimora per l'agire: Dimensioni ecclesiologiche della morale* (Rome: PUL-Mursia, 2000) pp. 73-97
———, 'Il pensiero personalista nella Grecia del secolo XX: Un primo tentativo di sintesi', in G. Grandi (ed), *L'idea di persona nel pensiero orientale* (Soveria Mannelli: Rubbettino, 2003) pp. 37-75
———, 'Christos Yannaras e i sacri canoni: Una parabola ermeneutica', in Congregazione per le Chiese Orientali, *Ius Ecclesiarum Vehiculum Caritatis:*

Atti del simposio internazionale per il decennale dell'enrtata in vigore del Codex Canonum Ecclesiarum Orientalium (Vatican City: Libreria Editrice Vaticana, 2004) pp. 921-39

———, 'Christos Yannaras (1935-)', *Credere oggi* 24, no. 2 (2004), pp. 121-30

———, 'Ecclesialità ed etica Cristiana: Annotazioni sul pensiero di Ch. Yannaras e Y. Zizioulas', *Nicolaus* 30, nos 1-2 (2003) [published in 2004], pp. 203-17

———, 'Personalist Thought in Greece in the Twentieth Century: A First Tentative Synthesis', *The Greek Orthodox Theological Review* 50, nos 1-4 (2005), pp. 2-48

———, 'Yannaras, Christos', in A. Pavan (ed), *Enciclopedia della persona nel XX secolo* (Naples: Edizioni Scientifiche Italiane, 2008) pp. 1127-34

———, 'Christos Yannaras: *Un'introduzione alla sua vita e al suo pensiero*', in Christos Yannaras, *Ontologia delle relazione*, ed. with an essay by Basilio Petrà (Troina [En]: Citta Aperta, 2010) pp. 7-27

———, *L'etica ortodossa: Storia, fonti, identità* (Assisi: Cittadella, 2010) passim

———, 'Preface' to Ch. Yannaras, *Contro la religione* (Magnano: Qiqajon [Community of Bose], 2012) pp. 5-16

———, 'Christos Yannaras and the Idea of "Dysis"', in George E. Demacopoulos and Aristotle Papanikolaou (eds), *Orthodox Constructions of the West* (New York: Fordham University Press, 2013) pp. 161-80

Polychronidis, Ath., 'Hoi theologikes syntetagmenes tōn neuroepistēmōn: Paradeigmatikes anaphores ston John Eccles kai Chrēsto Giannara' (The theological coordinates of the neurosciences: Paradigmatic references to John Eccles and Christos Yannaras), dissertation under the direction of Prof. Ioannis Kourempeles, School of Theology – Department of Theology, dogmatic theology section, Aristotle University of Thessaloniki, 2010

Prevelakis, N., 'Theologies as Alternative Histories: John Romanides and Chrestos Yannaras', *Classic@Online Journal*, Issue 10 (2014), at ///H:/Classic@10%20 %20Nicolas%20Prevelakis,%20Theologies%20as%20Alternative%20 Histories%20%20John%20Romanides%20and%20Chrestos%20Yannaras.htm

Ramphos, S., *Ho Kaēmos tou Henos: Kephalaia tēs psychikēs historias tōn Hellēnōn* (Athens: Harmos, 2000); English translation by Norman Russell under the title, Stelios Ramfos, *Yearning for the One: Chapters in the Inner Life of the Greeks* (Brookline, MA: Holy Cross Orthodox Press, 2011)

Ranson, Père Patric, *La doctrine des néo-orthodoxes sur l'amour* (Paris: Fraternité Orthodoxe Saint Grégoire Palamas, 1990)

Russell, N., 'Modern Greek Theologians and the Greek Fathers', *Philosophy and Theology* 18, no. 1 (2006), pp. 77-92

———, 'Christos Yannaras (1935-) and Panayiotis Nellas (1936-1986) – Transcending Created Finitude', in Ernst M. Conradie (ed), *Creation and Salvation, Volume 2: A Companion on Recent Theological Movements* (Berlin: LIT Verlag, 2012) pp. 51-55

———, 'Christos Yannaras', in Staale Johannes Kristiansen and Svein Rise (eds), *Key Theological Thinkers: From Modern to Postmodern* (Farnham: Ashgate, 2013) pp. 725-34

———, 'The Enduring Significance of Christos Yannaras: Some Further Works in Translation', *International Journal for the Study of the Christian Church* 16, no. 1 (2016), pp. 58-65

Spiteris, Y., *La teologia ortodossa neo-greca* (Bologna: EDB, 1992)
Stoeckl, K., *Community after Totalitarianism: The Russian Orthodox Intellectual Tradition and the Philosophical Discourse of Political Modernity* (Frankfurt: Peter Lang, 2008)
——— , 'Contemporary Orthodox Discourses on Human Rights: The Standpoint of Christos Yannaras in a Political Philosophical Perspective', in Evert van der Zweerde and Alfons Brüning (eds), *Orthodox Christianity and Human Rights* (Louvain: Peeters, 2012) pp. 185-99
——— , 'Post-Secular Subjectivity in Western Philosophy and Eastern Orthodox Thought', in David Bradshaw (ed), *Philosophical Theology and the Christian Traditions: Russian and Western Perspectives* (Washington, D.C.: The Council for Research in Values and Philosophy, 2012) pp. 187-97
Sumares, M., 'Signifying the Mystical as Struggle: Yannaras' Orthodox Refiguring of Philosophy of Language', *Annals of the University of Bucharest, Philosophy Series* 63, no. 1 (2014), pp. 3-15
——— , 'Apofatismo e Estatuto Ontológico da Igreja: O Contributo de Christos Yannaras para a Recuperação da Racionalidade Remanescente da Ortodoxia', *Comunio: Revista Internacional Católica* 32, no. 4 (2015), pp. 419-32
Swinburne, R., 'A Response to Christos Yannaras' *Against Religion*', *Oxbridge Philokalic Review* 2 (2013), pp. 54-60
Tănase, N., 'Otherness and Apophaticism: Yannaras' Discourse of "Personhood" and the Apophatic Theognosia', *Philotheos* 14 (2014), pp. 254-67
Theoklitos Dionysiatis monachos, *Ho nikolaïtikos erōtismos tōn neorthodoxōn (me theorētiko ton k. Giannara)* (The Nicolaitic eroticism of the neo-Orthodox [with Mr Yannaras as its theoretician]) (Athens: Orthodoxos Typos, 1989)
Ventis, H., 'Political Constructivism and Ontology: John Rawls' Freestanding Political Conception versus Liberal and Religious Comprehensive Doctrines' (in Greek), *Theologia* 74 (2003), pp. 281-313
Voloudakis, V.E., *Orthodoxia kai Ch. Giannaras* (Orthodoxy and Ch. Yannaras) (Athens: Hypakoē, 1993)
Ware, K., 'Scholasticism and Orthodoxy: Theological Method as a Factor in the Schism', *Eastern Churches Review* 5, no. 1 (1973), pp. 16-27
Williams, R.D., 'The Theology of Personhood: A Study of the Thought of Christos Yannaras', *Sobornost* (1st series) 6, no. 6 (1972), pp. 415-16
Zouboulakis, S., 'To "Synoro" kai ho Chrēstos Giannaras: Hē theologikē protasē tēs apoēthikopoiēsēs tou Christianismou' ('Synoro' and Christos Yannaras: The theological proposition of the de-ethicisation of Christianity), in P. Kalaitzidis, Th.N. Papathanasiou and Th. Ampatzidis (eds), *Anataraxeis stē metapolemikē theologia: Hē 'Theologia tou '60'*, pp. 315-26

Index

adaequatio rei et intellectus, 51
Adorno, T., 53, 54n.57
Ahura Mazda, 112
Aktines, journal, 2n.6
Allchin, A.M., 35n.4
Allport, G., 2n.6
Androutsos, C., 16n.6
anti-Westernism, 28n.37, 29-30, 82
apologetics, rationalist, 30-1
apophaticism, Eastern, 19, 21, 30-3, 35; philosophical, 58-61, 64-5, 103-8; Western, 17, 18-19, 31
Aquinas, St Thomas, 9, 38n.19
Aristotle, 99, 103n18, 105
art, religious, 85
Aspiotis, A.A., 2, 6n.18
Augustine, 69n.106
authoritarianism, 29
Baruk, H., 2n.6
Basil the Great, St, 19, 38n.16, 73-4
beauty, 78-9, 97
Being, 17, 41, 56
Berdyaev, N., 2, 3-4, 5, 8
Binswanger, L., 2n.6
Bohr, N., 32
Briere, E., 49n.42
Bulgakov, S., 8

Camus, A., 9-10
Carnap, R., 33n52, 59
Caruso, I., 2
Castoriadis, C., 54, 76n.26
Cavafy, C.P., 50n.48
Christ, person of, 46, 47, 112
Christianity, 111-12
Church, 47-8, 88-9, 112
Clément, O., 4, 10, 16n.6
communion (*koinōnia*), 20, 22, 42, 46, 47, 98-101, 109
Concilium, journal, viii
consciousness, 78
deification, 20-1
democracy, 63, 109-10
Democritus, 26
Descartes, R., 9
Deukalion, journal, 35
dimotiki, viin.2
Dionysius the Areopagite, St, 16, 19, 20, 21, 39n.19, 43, 104
distantiality (*apostasē*), 42n.28, 43, 47
Dostoevsky, F., 5-10, 14, 18, 82
Eccles, J., 66
ecumenicity, 13
ek-stasē, 37, 38, 40
empiricism, 68, 100

energies, divine, 20, 38
Enlightenment, 9, 53
epistemology, 59
Epoches, journal, 4
eros, 40, 100
essence, divine, 20
Evdokimov, P., 8
evil, 5, 79
Fall, 6n.18, 40, 43-6, 47, 79-80
Feyerabend, P., 59
Florensky, P., 8
Florovsky, G., 8
Frankfurt School, 55
Frankl, V., 2n.6
freedom, 3, 5, 40, 45n.36, 56, 61-5, 67, 70n.107, 112
Freud, S., 54
gnoseology, 24, 25n.29, 30, 32-3, 59, 100, 110-12
God, 25n.30, 31, 112; death of, 9, 16n.6, 17-18, 86
grace, 48
Gregory of Nyssa, St, 19
Gregory Palamas, St, 19, 38
Gregory the Theologian, St, 19
Habermas, J., 52n.51, 53, 55, 63
Hayek, F. von, 62
Hegel, G.W.F., 17
Heidegger, M., 14, 15-25, 28, 30, 35, 37, 40, 41, 42, 43-5, 72n.4, 75, 81, 86, 105
Heisenberg, W., 32
hell, 45n.36, 46
Hellenism, viii, 27n.34, 50, 92, 105, 111
Heraclitus, 97-8, 104, 105
hesychasm, 13, 88
Horkheimer, M., 53, 54n.57
Husserl, E., 37n.14
iconoclasm, 12
ideology, 3
individualism, 3, 29
Irenaeus of Samos, metropolitan, 3n.8
Isaac the Syrian, St, 43
Jevtic, A., 35n.4
John Climacus, St, 34n.2
John Damascene, St, 19

Kalaitzidis, P., 13, 28n.37
Kant, I., 17, 52-3, 54, 55
Karamazov, Alyosha, 6
katharevousa, viin.2
Kathēmerinē, newspaper 4, 7
Khomiakov, A., 8
Kierkegaard, S., 75
knowledge, 76, 96-8
Kourouklis, C., 34n2
Koutroubis, D., 2, 4, 5, 34n2
Kuhn, T., 59
Lacan, J., 28, 56, 57, 58, 62, 69, 76-80
Lakatos, I., 59
language, philosophy of, 33, 72-6, 94, 101-4
legalism, 29
Lersch, P., 2n.6
libido, 76, 77
Lorentzatos, Z., 5, 32n47
Lossky, V., 4-5, 8, 10, 19, 35-6, 38n.18, 43n.30
Loudovikos, N., 37n.14
love, 48
Makriyannis, Y., 11
Marcuse, H., 53
Marx, K., 9, 28, 53, 55, 56-7, 58, 62, 63-4, 65-6
Maximus the Confessor, St, 19, 43, 46
metaphysics, possibility of, 50
Meyendorff, J., 8
monasticism, 12n.41
moralism, 35
nature, 39
Nietzsche, F., 9, 14, 17, 22, 86, 105
nihilism, 14, 18, 19-20, 21, 22, 28, 30, 35
Nikodemos the Hagiorite, St, 29
Nissiotis, N., 19, 32
ontology, viiin.3, 16, 22, 24n.27, 25n.29, 27-8, 51-2; critical, 49, 50, 55-6, 65-70; erroneous, 82-3; relational, 77-80; and salvation, 81-3
Orthodox Theological Research Forum (ORTF), viiin.4
Orthodoxism, 88, 90

Orthodoxy, Greek, 10-13; mission of, 6, 8, 11-12; Russian, 8; and the West, 29-30
Palamas, Gregory, *see* Gregory Palamas, St
Papadiamantis, A., 11
Panteion University, viiin.3
participation, 97, 100-1, 107, 111; *see also* communion (*koinōnia*)
Pascal, B., 105
person, personalism, 2, 5, 34-52, 70n.107; definition of, 36
Petrà, B., 2n.4, 25n.30, 49n.42, 50n.47
Philokalia, 11, 90-1
philosophy, genesis of, 94
pietism, 2, 12, 29
Pikionis, D., 5
Plato, 100
polis (city-state), 106-8
politics, 107-8
Popper, K., 28, 33n52, 49n.43, 55, 59, 62, 66
positivism, logical, 33, 54, 59, 73
progress, ideology of, 54n.57
prosōpo (person), 4-5, 26, 42; *see also* person, personalism
Protestantism, 7
Putnam, H., 59
Quine, W., 59
rationalism, 52-65; apophatic, 58
relation, 27, 36, 41-2, 56-7, 62, 67-8, 74-80, 100; erotic, 78
relativity, theory of, 32
religion, *see threskeiopoiēsē* ('religionisation')
Romanides, J.S., 28n.38
Russia, 6n.16, 7n.23
sacraments, 48, 89
salvation, economy of, 43, 46, 47; of the West, 82
Sartre, J.-P., 14n.50, 23, 28, 39, 43-5
schism, of 1054, 28, 85; philosophical, 50
Schmemann, A., 8
Schneider, K., 2n.6
scientism, 54
self-awareness (*autepignosē*), 66-7

Seraphim of Sarov, St, 9, 11
Sextus Empiricus, 98n.10
sexuality, 77-8
Sherrard, P., 35n.4
Skapanē, journal, 1n.1, 6n.18
Slavophiles, 8-9
societas, 109
Socrates, 108
Solomos, D., 11
Sorbonne, 1
Stavrou, M., 28n.38
symbol, 74, 101-3
Synoro, journal, 1n.1
Tarski, A., 59
Terzakis, A., 4, 14n.50
theology, relationship to philosophy, 43
thrēskeiopoiēsē ('religionisation'), 83-90
time, 41n.23
totalitarianism, 54
Touraille, J., 16n.6
Tournier, P., 2
truth, 58, 94, 96-8, 99, 106, 109, 111
utilitarianism, 95, 98-9, 105, 108, 109
verification, communal, 99, 104; critical, 52, 68-9, 70n.107, 108, 111
Weber, M., 28, 52n.51, 53
West, the 4, 5-9, 13, 27-30, 82-3, 89, 91, 105; *see also thrēskeiopoiēsē* ('religionisation')
Williams, R.D., 35n.4
Wittgenstein, L., 28, 31, 59, 72-5, 105
Yannaras, Christos, biographical matter, 1-5, 15-16, 71-2, 81-2, 84-6; quoted passages, *Against Religion*, 88-91; *Hē apologētikē sta horia tēs orthodoxou theologias*, 30-3; *Hē kokkinē plateia kai ho theios Arthouros*, 84-5; *Hē Neoellēnikē tautotēta*, 27n.34; *Kritikes Parembaseis*, 49n.43; *Mia synenteuxē*, 28n.38; *On the Absence and Unknowability of God*, 16-21, 86-7; 'Orthodoxy and the West',

29; *Orthos logos kai koinōnikē praktikē*, 52-65; *Person and Eros*, 14, 34-49, 51, 70n.107; *Politistikē diplomatia*, 26-7; *Protaseis kritikēs ontologias*, 65-9; *Relational Ontology*, 77-80; *Ta kath' eauton*, 15, 22-3; 'The communal verification of knowledge', 94-112; *The Enigma of Evil*, 24n.27; *The Freedom of Morality*, 10; *The Schism in Philosophy*, 23n.26, 25nn.29-30, 43n.31; *Timioi me tēn Orthodoxia*, 7-13; *To rhēto kai to arrhēto*, 50, 71-7

Zander, V., 8

Zeus, 112

Zizioulas, J., 25-7

Zōē movement 1, 3, 5, 6, 7

Zouboulakis, S., 1n.1, 2n.3

The Inhumanity of Right
Christos Yannaras
Translated by Norman Russell

Christos Yannaras' pioneering critique of the concept of the right of the individual is presented in English for the first time. This central aspect of political theory (since Hegel's Philosophy of Right) summarizes the philosophical and cultural identity of the paradigm of modernity, but the philosophical assumptions underlying the concept of right have not hitherto been subject to scrutiny. Yannaras shows that the starting-point of the concept of right is a phenomenalistic naturalism, which presupposes an abstract concept of the human subject as a fundamentally undifferentiated natural individual. The question is also explored of how the priority accorded to this concept of right is related to the contemporary crisis of the modern politico-social paradigm, while a new preface from the translator underlines the continued significance of Yannaras' proposal for Anglophone readers.

Against the modern concept of right with its illusion of objectivity, *The Inhumanity of Right* sketches out the basic lines of a political theory that prioritizes new social needs that reflect the relational character of the human person.

Christos Yannaras, Emeritus Professor of Philosophy at the Panteion University of Athens, has been proclaimed 'without doubt the most important living Greek Orthodox theologian' (Andrew Louth), 'contemporary Greece's greatest thinker' (Olivier Clément), and 'one of the most significant Christian philosophers in Europe' (Rowan Williams).

Norman Russell is Honorary Research Fellow of St Stephen's House, University of Oxford. He is well known as a patristics scholar and translator from Greek, Italian, and French. An experienced interpreter of Yannaras's thinking, he has already translated seven of his works.

Specifications: 234x156mm / 180pp / Published: 2021
Hardback ISBN: 978 0 227 17754 9 / Paperback ISBN: 978 0 227 17755 6 /
PDF ISBN: 978 0 227 90753 5 / ePub ISBN: 978 0 227 90754 2 / Kindle ISBN: 978 0 227 90753 5

POLIS, ONTOLOGY, ECCLESIAL EVENT
Engaging with Christos Yannaras' Thought
edited by Sotiris Mitralexis

Christos Yannaras is seen as 'the most important living Greek Orthodox theologian' (Andrew Louth), 'contemporary Greece's greatest thinker' (Olivier Clément), 'one of the most significant Christian philosophers' (Rowan Williams).

Despite this, the bulk of his work is only now being translated. The present volume explores aspects of Yannaras' contributions to Orthodox theology, philosophy and political thought, based on his relational ontology of the person, later popularised in the Anglophone sphere by John Zizioulas. From political theology to Heidegger and the philosophy of language, from Yannaras' critique of religion to the patristic grounding of the theology of the person, this volume comprises a panorama of Christos Yannaras' transdisciplinary contributions.

Sotiris Mitralexis is Seeger Fellow at Princeton University, Assistant Professor of philosophy at the City University of Istanbul and Visiting Research Fellow at the University of Winchester.

Specifications: 234x156mm / 278pp / Published: 2018
Hardback ISBN: 978 0 227 17669 6 / Paperback ISBN: 978 0 227 17671 9 /
PDF ISBN: 978 0 227 90645 3 / ePub ISBN: 978 0 227 90646 0 / Kindle ISBN: 978 0 227 90647 7

EVER-MOVING REPOSE
A Contemporary Reading of
Maximus the Confessor's Theory of Time
Sotiris Mitralexis

A contemporary exploration at Maximus the Confessor's (580-662) understanding of temporality, logoi, and deification, through the perspective of Christos Yannaras, as well as John Zizioulas and Nicholas Loudovikos. Mitralexis shows that Maximus possesses both a unique theological ontology and a unique threefold theory of temporality: time, the Aeon, and the radical transformation of temporality and motion in an ever-moving repose. These three distinct modes of temporality enable reconstruction of a Maximian theory of time, manifesting a perfect communion-in-otherness. In examining Maximian temporality, the author not only focusses on one aspect of Maximus' comprehensive Weltanschauung, but looks at the Maximian vision as a whole through the lens of temporality and motion.

Sotiris Mitralexis is Seeger Fellow at Princeton University, Assistant Professor of philosophy at the City University of Istanbul and Visiting Research Fellow at the University of Winchester.

Specifications: 229x15mm / 256pp / Published: 2018
Paperback ISBN: 978 0 227 17684 9 / PDF ISBN: 978 0 227 90680 4